Reckless to Restored

Written by: Ashia Bruton

Acknowledgments

To my mother **Velva Theresa Bruton-Cooper**, I thank you for being an amazing and loving mother to my sister and I in the short amount of time that we had with you. It is because of you that I am the mother that I am today.

To my cousin **Charmaine Clark**, thank you for being more than just a cousin to me but more like a second mother, cousin, and best friend all in one. You were always there to listen to me and give me sound advice based on the path that you had already traveled upon and for that I am eternally grateful to you!

To my **Aunie**, thank you for your protection and guidance. You raised me after my mom passed away and gave up your dreams to do it. It is because of you that I am the strong independent woman that I am today.

To my **Grandpa,** thank you for investing your time into me. I didn't understand growing up why you were so invested in me more than your other grandchildren, but today I have come to realize that you recognized my greatness and until you took your last breath you were determined to see me put my gifts into the earth.

Last, but certainly not least I want to say thank you to my **Grandmother** for being the strong black woman that you were to our family. I stand on your shoulders and I proudly carry on your legacy and I reproduce and try to be an even greater woman to my children as you were to yours.

I stand on the shoulders of all of you and the ancestors who came before me that I never got to know . I only wish to birth my knowledge, expertise, and gifts into the earth so that you know your lives and struggles were not in vain!

Contents

Introduction

The things discussed in this book may not be for everyone, but for someone, it will mean the difference between life and death metaphorically speaking. Meaning you may be in a situation right now, that you feel you can NEVER overcome due to the obstacles and challenges seeming insurmountable! However, it is my hope that through the transparency shared in this book, you gain a new perspective on life. That through my hardships and struggles discussed, two things happen for you: you learn that you do not have to endure the same trials and errors that I endured; and that you're not alone. Your situation is not an isolated situation. Somewhere in the world someone else is either dealing with the same situation, overcoming it, or like myself has gone through it. *"Resist him, firm in your faith, knowing that the same kinds of suffering are being experienced by your brotherhood throughout the world 1Peter 5:9".*

I want you to know that you can stand on my shoulders as you climb into your destiny that God has for your life. I have made the errors and while doing so, I lacked access to the information that could have freed me and allowed me to do things differently. However, you now have access to the information that could change your life and alter your circumstances.

Writing this book was not easy for me because I was not comfortable with sharing intimate details of my life with the world. However, a small still voice on the inside of me said *that the pain along my journey in life was not meant for me to carry, it was meant for me to share so that someone else could receive a breakthrough.* I endured the pain so that I could be an inspiration to someone else in my situation.

As I get ready to enter into the best phase of my life, it is my calling and life's duty to take you through my journey to show you the inner source that lives within you, is for you, and is always wanting the best for you.

God is such an amazing and merciful divine entity. Through the process of learning who you are, you will ultimately discover your inner source and the universe's plans for your life. God is patient and therefore, you should be patient with yourself through the good and bad times in life.

We have all been at a point in our lives where we have felt lost. You may be lost at this very moment, while you're reading this book, but I hope that at the conclusion or even in the midst of reading this book that something within you resonates with what I am saying and you begin to have a shift in your thinking that will cause you to want something different for yourself. Yes, you do have a purpose in your life. You were not created in vain or by mistake.

Each one of us was born with potential and purpose in this world; however, throughout our existence, we have endured pain and trauma, which has caused us to be distracted and redirected from our potential and purpose in life. We are our biggest critic and enemy. If we are not careful, we can self-destruct and end up stuck trying to pick up the pieces from the damage in which we have allowed.

At 33 years old, I am beginning to discover my purpose and my life will never be the same! My purpose is to help people like you. The biggest misconception about God is that you must come in perfect form in order to be accepted and walk in purpose. Who told us those lies? Our inner source or the place in which God resides within us does not remember or keep a record of what happened in the past. It only knows the present and the future. We hold ourselves hostage from our future by not forgiving ourselves for past hurts, traumas, and pain. Truth is pain is a necessary process in this human experience. Pain helps to push us further into destiny. It is only through pain and disappointment that you can discover what you do not want out of life and discover what it is that you do want and desire.

I hope that you find encouragement through reading this book and that it inspires you to seek out your inner source and discover the ultimate plan for your life! You are unique and needed on earth to help someone or to do something extraordinary. Do not allow the pain, abuse, trauma, stigma, rumors, mistakes, etc. to deter you from your destiny. Get back up, dust yourself off, be inspired, and seek the knowledge necessary to bring back the fire that lives within you to do the things in which you were created to do here on earth. The world needs YOU!

You can read all the chapters of this book except for _Recklessly Losing Pieces of my Soul_. This was my most VULNERABLE chapter.

Reckless: Beginning

In November 2007 my life changed forever! It was a regular day at work, and I decided to call and make a doctor's appointment for a pain that I was having at the bottom of my stomach. To my surprise, the doctor ran some tests, came back into the room, and said "Congratulations Ms. Bruton you're pregnant". Pregnant??? No, that could not be right. I had been trying for over five years to become pregnant and had given up on the notion that I could become pregnant. So, I replied, "Are you sure? I don't think you guys have the right patient." She said, "Oh yes, we are sure. We ran the test several times and it comes back positive."

As I walked out to the car of my soon-to-be child's father he asks, "what's wrong with you? What you find out you were pregnant or something"?

As he is laughing, I replied "yes," as I hand him the paper that estimated how far along, I was and my predicted due date. He had wanted us to have a child for years, so this news was the best news that he could have received. He knew how bad I wanted to be a mom, and he would always tell me that I was going to make a good mom one day.

Meanwhile, I was still in disbelief. I had so many thoughts going through my head. What if I miscarry? What if I wake up and this is all a dream, and this isn't even real? Am I ready to be someone's mother? Ready or not, this was happening. I was getting ready to become someone's mother and responsible for them for the rest of my life.

I was 23 when I found out that I was pregnant, and I understood who God was, but I did not have an inner relationship with God. So many of my thoughts were worldly and not spiritual. Had I had a relationship with God and understood divinity then I would have been jumping for joy because I had manifested my pregnancy from a thought into my reality.

See God speaks to us all the time thru visions, dreams, prophecy, signs, and symbols; but we must be quiet enough to see them and to hear them when he speaks. I had dreams of a little girl several times before I became pregnant, but I just dismissed them as being dreams when they were actually God letting me know that a child was not only my want but was a part of the plan for my life.

The vibrations of what I wanted for my life were met with the desire of what God wanted for my life causing alignment and manifestation to become my physical reality. Wherever we focus our energy we have the power to manifest it into our existence whether it be good or bad. It's call the Law of Attraction. What I did not know was that this child was only the beginning of what God had planned for my life over the next several years.

There was a transformation getting ready to take place that if I were asked to do voluntarily, I would have declined. Who wants to be hurt, struggle, go without, lose possessions, etc., in order to grasp a concept or learn a lesson? However, change can only occur when we are uncomfortable in our situations. Little did I know I was getting ready to embark on a journey like Noah, Abraham, Moses, Jonah, Job, and Ruth to name just a few.

See, I must take you guys back a little further into the past before I can bring you forward; for you to utterly understand the beauty of my transformation.

I was born to two teenagers straight out of high school. My mother was 19 and my father 18. My mom had my brother when she was 13 or 14, but I believe her body was not fully developed and that played a role in the developmental challenges of my brother. He died a little after his first birthday. Had he been alive today, I would have a 38 or 39-year-old big brother ☺. My parents being teenagers and still trying to figure out life, did not end up raising me together. I remember my dad would come over to visit us when we lived in the projects and somewhere around me being the age of four or five, my mom met my stepfather. He was always nice to me and my sister. Oh yeah my mom ended up having another baby two years after I was born. So, at the age of 21, she had given birth to three children and had two who survived.

I remember I was about five when we moved out of the projects and into a cute black and white house. It was also where I would have my first neurological experiences with trauma as I witnessed domestic violence at an early age. I remember hearing my mom and stepdad get into arguments and hearing him beating on her.

I recall one New Year's Eve; they had gone out and when they came back home, they were arguing. I was happy my mom was home, so I got out of bed and was on my way to her room. However, when I got into the hallway, their door was open, and I stood and watched my stepdad as he punched my mom, knocking her into the dresser and then her falling and hitting the floor. What I did not realize at that time was that my stepfather was an abusive alcoholic and his disease caused our family a lifetime of pain. I still am healing from what was absorbed into my psyche at a young and vulnerable age.

I must have heard lots of fights because I recall being in elementary school and whenever I would hold my spoon to eat food my hands would shake bad. One day, the counselor took me into their office and he or she was asking me several questions. I think they thought that I was being abused at home. However, had they asked about my mom, perhaps they could have saved us, as I would have told them what I knew, but as a five-year-old, you typically only give answers to what you're being asked. At least I did anyway.

The fights continued and I remember one day, my stepdad came to pick me up from school. He asked if my biological dad had been in our car and I replied yes. My stepdad had recently got us a red Nissan Sentra. My mom and one of my aunts were on their way up to my school to come and pick me up, but my stepdad had beat them. Upon my mom getting home, my stepdad ended up beating her up as he suspected that my mom was having an affair with my dad. My mom ended up going to the clinic where another one of my aunts worked to get checked out for a fractured arm as well as her tooth that had been chipped.

As I write this book, those same feelings of sadness and sorrow arise in me today, just as they did back then. Like most domestic violence victims, the multiple beatings, fractured arm, and broken tooth were not enough for my mother to leave. Many people look at women in domestic violence relationships as being weak or stupid. However, domestic violence is not only physical but mental abuse as well. My mother saw and or heard her mother be a victim of domestic violence by my grandfather and that exposure, in turn, internalized to the point in which she found abuse to be comfortable. The abuse seemed familiar to her. So, therefore, when she experienced abuse, she did not leave the situation because it felt familiar to her.

Women who find themselves in domestic violence relationships are often terrified to leave due to the repercussions they are likely to face. Often, many women do not make it out alive. I cannot tell you how many times I have heard the line 'If you're not going to be with me then you're not going to be with anybody'.

Another reason women stay in these sorts of relationships is due to the abuser being a master manipulator. The women find themselves caught in what is called the 'Blame Cycle'. There is a fight/argument, the abuser apologizes stating they will never harm the victim again, they do nice things for the victim, there is a period of calm, and then something upsets the abuser and the cycle starts again.

In most cases, the woman ends up becoming co-dependent in the relationship as she feels sorry for him. She knows that he needs help, she believes that if she leaves him, he will be worse off, and the abuser often manipulates her by stating that if she leaves he will harm himself, making it harder for her to walk away. My mom happened to be one of those women and she returned to my stepdad only for the beatings to continue.

We moved from the Westside to the Eastside where the majority of our family resided. I believe my mother was trying to leave my stepfather because he did not move with us into this apartment. He would come over and try to get in by banging at the door. However, my mom stood her ground and would not let him.

I am writing this at the age of 33 and recalling these things from the age of five. So I don't recall exactly how it happened, but I believe that after the last big fight where my mom's arm was fractured and her tooth broken that the police must have been called and the state picked up the charges because my stepfather ended up going to prison. I remember going to the prison to visit him with my mom, but at that time not realizing we were at a state prison facility.

During his incarceration, my mom left for work one morning, it was during the wintertime and the roads were icy. Her car ended up spinning out on black ice as a semi-truck was coming. The truck driver did not have enough time to stop and he ended up hitting her car. She was on life support for a couple of weeks with crushed ribs and unable to breathe on her own. The doctors informed the family of her condition and the decision was made to pull the plug. This happened in the early '90s and back then the prison for a small fee allowed my stepfather to come to the funeral before anyone else was in there and say his goodbyes to my mom. My aunt said the sounds of sorrow, pain, and heartache she heard from my stepfather she had never heard in her life. I believe that there was also a lot of regret in those tears. He would never be able to show her if he changed or to apologize to her as they learned to be

7

friends and as they grew and got to know themselves as individuals. All those things were gone, and he would now have to live with the regret of his actions.

I was six years old when my mom passed away. I was in the first grade. My mom had just taken out a life insurance policy and left my aunt as the beneficiary and our sole custodian. However, since my biological father was still living, he had to sign over his parental rights before she could gain custody. He signed them over willingly, no fight whatsoever. I remember him coming over to her house to sign the papers and me showing him my room as he carried me up the stairs.

I never saw him again until I was 17 years old. I later realized God will never take someone out of your life without replacing them with someone else. My aunt lived right across the street from my grandparents. My uncle lived in the back of my grandparents. My favorite oldest cousin lived a couple of streets over and by the time I was in high school she ended up moving on the same street as my aunt and grandparents and got a house right next door to my aunt, which was her mother. So, I grew up with lots of family; but the most important person being my grandfather.

My grandmother had seven children. However, only three of them were by my grandfather, and that was my mom and my two uncles. After my grandfather lost his only daughter, he held on tight to me and my sister. When I tell you, I was spoiled by my grandfather that word is an understatement. That man would climb to the sky just to pick out the star I wanted if I would have asked him too. He was my best friend, my father, spiritual advisor, he was my everything.

I spent so much time listening to stories he would tell me, and he spent lots of time bragging about me to anyone who would or would not listen. That included family, the mailman, the bank teller, and his masonic brothers… lol. Anyone. I was an As and Bs student all through school and when it came time for college, I applied to The Ohio State University, The University of Cincinnati, as well as Capital University, and I got accepted to each of them! If you are not familiar with these colleges, let me just say they are all exceptionally good colleges! I did not grow up in a home where anyone had gone to college. So, although my grandfather was excited, I did not have anyone taking me on college tours, helping me decide which is the best college to attend, what would be a reasonable college to afford, etc.

I had one cousin who was in college, but she was in her early 20s and raising a child. Had I asked her she would have helped me, but at that time in her life, she was still trying to figure out life for herself. The point I am making is it did not feel like a big deal to me. Okay, I was on the honor roll every quarter, big deal, and I was inducted into the National Honors society. Yes, I got accepted into AWESOME colleges, I thought they sent those letters to everyone.

It was not until I became a mother and started looking back on my life that I realized the things that I had passed up on. I realized the little girl that lived within me who was looking for validation and the approval of her parents. That little girl wanted to know that she was loved, cared for, and most importantly that she was SAFE. However, because those needs were not met the teenage version of myself couldn't validate and celebrate successes and therefore, the opportunity to attend awesome colleges was lost.

In addition to that, I did not have anyone explaining to me the importance of what was transpiring in my life or how hard my life would become by turning down those opportunities that were given to me. Not because they did not want to tell me, but how do you explain to someone the importance of academics when you didn't finish 8th grade, or you didn't graduate, or you barely graduated? They could not explain these things to me simply because they just did not know!! They lacked access to this information!

My grandfather was very adamant about me going to college. I did not understand why back then, but looking back now, I understand that for his bloodline I would have been a first-generation college attendee.

I've recently been doing some family research and found that going back to my ancestors on my grandfather's side, after slavery, they worked to better themselves, and in doing so they valued education, by sending their children onto school. Today that does not sound like a big deal, but it was for them. To be able to afford to send your children to school rather than to have them out working on a farm, meant that the family was well off or made a sacrifice of having less in order for their children to have a better life. My ancestors probably had no idea that the sacrifices that they made back then would impact their grandchildren several generations later.

As I am writing this, I have a newfound appreciation for their sacrifices that they made back then on making education important. On the flip side, my grandmother did not have the opportunity to attend school due to having to help around the house with chores, her siblings, and picking tobacco on a farm in North Carolina to help support her family. This was very typical for African American families back in that period, so for my ancestors on my grandfather's side to be able to afford to have their children attend school rather than work was a BIG deal for that period and it spoke volumes about their mindset back then. They had no idea that they were setting the precedence not only for their children but for their great-grandchildren to come.

Often in life, our parental skills are based on the knowledge in which those who raised us were equipped unless you purposely seek after additional knowledge beyond what you were given.

See life is funny and there is this thing called 'Generational Curses'. If you are not aware of them then they can easily attach themselves to you and you will find yourself bound by them. Simply put our children pick up our habits, traditions, mannerisms, etc., good or bad, and they pass them along from one generation to the next and unless they are taught that something is incorrect it continues to be passed down through the bloodline.

My grandmother before giving birth to my mother had been in several domestic violence relationships and when she met my grandfather and got pregnant with my mother, the abuse did not stop, but it continued with him as well. Lo and behold, my mother did not ask, nor did she want to be abused, but found herself in the same cycle. In fact, all my grandmother's daughters at some point in their lives were in a domestic violence relationship.

So, here I was at the age of 17 getting ready to embark down the same path as my elders and did not even know it. I graduated from high school and had decided I was going to take a break from school. I was dating this street guy who was in and out of the juvenile detention center and back then I was attracted to street guys. I found guys who went to school or were doing the right thing to be so boring and unattractive.

My grandfather was so upset with me and heartbroken that I was not going to college. He felt I was throwing away my life to be with this 'thug', rather than go away to college and make something of myself and add even more value to the family lineage. Looking back, it was as if God made a promise or showed my grandfather that I was the chosen one. I say that because my grandfather had such different expectations for me than he did for his children and even his other grandchildren.

Well, instead of making my grandfather proud, I ended up moving out and getting my own apartment. That is when life got REAL!!! I was working and my boyfriend was coming by whenever he was not out being a menace to society and sleeping around with other females.

So, I recall one evening getting a call from a guy that I use to date off and on in high school asking if he could come over and see me. Hey, why not? So, he comes over, we talk, we laugh, and kick it for a little bit and then we fall asleep. I remember waking up because I could feel someone staring at me. When I opened my eyes, I found my 'boyfriend' staring at me. The next thing I know, he is slapping me, punching me, and calling me all sorts of explicit names. The guy who was there with me does not even try to interject himself to stop me from getting beat up; he gets up and leaves my apartment. The part I was most puzzled by was how my boyfriend who had *no* key to my apartment got into the house.

Once the police came, they explained to me how I am supposed to put the bar down on a patio door to secure it. I had never had a patio growing up, so I thought if the door is locked then it is locked. I was not aware that if the door is locked, but the bar is not down to secure it, someone could easily open the patio from the outside. (Just a little insight ladies in case your living in your first apartment right now as your reading this book.) I am still puzzled to this day as to how he got onto a second-floor balcony. I guess he had a little Spiderman in him…lol.

So, after that, I bet your reading this and saying, "Oh no, I would have left him". Right? But no, I did not. There were several other incidents where he came and beat me up and the beatings got a little worse each time. One time he went as far as to spit on me and kick me as if I were not a human life. The police would come and have him leave, yet they never arrested him. I do not even recall them asking me if I wanted to press charges.

I ended up having to move back home with my grandparents due to not being able to afford my rent at my apartment after being out on my own for a whole four months. My psycho boyfriend was still in my life and coming and going as he pleased.

Our drama continued as well. The beatings had ceased because he no longer had me alone and in an isolated situation. However, his control and sense of possession over me only escalated.

I remember one day as I was lying asleep on the couch I awoke to a noise. The next thing I know I open my eyes to see my on again off again boyfriend at the time crawling like a snake on the floor. He had somehow gotten into our side door, I was startled and wanted to scream, but he begged me not too and asked if we could just talk. As morning was quickly approaching, he knew my grandmother would be coming down the stairs. He knew he had to leave but wanted me to go with him. I did not want to go and so he literally picked me up and begins to carry me out the back door. At this point, I am screaming at the top of my lungs. My grandmother hears me, and she gets on the phone calling my aunt, cousin, and uncles. His mother stayed a couple of streets over and he is literally carrying me like a sack of potatoes over to his mother's house with me screaming for help all the way over there.

The next thing I know there were police and helicopters out looking for me. I believe someone in my family must have called the police and said that I had been kidnapped by my psycho boyfriend. When we got to his mom's house my aunt was driving down the street. When he saw her, he let me down and I was able to get into her car as she is literally ready to end his life. My family was way passed over him putting his hands on me and verbally abusing me. They say the apple does not fall too far from the tree. I remember as a teenager recalling my mom getting beat up and saying I would never let a man do the same thing to me. I had so much anger and hostility in me towards my stepdad for the things that he did to my mom and vowed that I would never let those things happen to me. However, it's easy to say what we will and won't do until we find ourselves in that same situation and then you fall in love, get your first boyfriend, and the lines of love and abuse get **REAL** blurry.

Wisdom rests in the heart of a man of understanding, but it makes itself known even in the midst of fools.
~Proverbs 14:33

Restored: Beginning

I would be doing you a disservice if I shared my story with you, but didn't share what I learned or give you some advice on how I would navigate through those situations today having learned and gained wisdom over the years. There is a verse in the Bible that states that just as your enduring trials and tribulations know that your brotherhood has also endured them as well. I am paraphrasing, but it's basically stating that nothing that we endure is an isolated situation. However, many times when we are in our situation we feel isolated and alone. Therefore, in my *Restored* sections of this book, I am letting you know that you are not alone and I am giving you advice on how to handle the situations that I shared in my *Reckless* chapters of this book. I didn't have the resources and tools during those periods of my life; however, now that I have gained the information and gotten out of those situations I am passing on my knowledge to you in hopes that it will help you to navigate more quickly and successfully through what you are going through.

I do not want this book to be a story of my life that you read and walk away saying oh that was a good book or oh wow she went through a lot. I want you to read this book and if something resonates with you it is my hope that I can provide you with some sort of inspiration, and or direction on how to deal with that situation in your own life.

So, in looking back over this chapter, someone should have definitely have put the younger me in some sort of counseling for children who have observed or been exposed to domestic violence. Even if counseling was something they could not afford, weren't aware of, or did not believe in, there should have been an adult to talk to me and help me to process my feelings and emotions of what I was seeing and experiencing. Those experiences created a trauma within me that got embedded into my subconscious and due to lack of guidance, I ended up attracting the very behavior I was afraid of into my adult life.

I grew up into an adult that internalized many thoughts and emotions. If you are in a domestic violence relationship with children, PLEASE put your children's needs first!! Children are defenseless in those situations and the effects on them are traumatic.

As a grown woman today in her 30s, I still suffer from showing emotion in my relationships. I am afraid to show emotion out of the fear of being hurt if I show vulnerability. So, in turn, my defense mechanism is to internalize emotions. I also still struggle with knowing what a healthy relationship looks and feels like because growing up I never saw one.

So, I am having to reconstruct what I knew and was taught growing up and teaching myself new behaviors and characteristics to keep myself safe. As a parent, if you have endured trauma whether it was in your childhood or your adult life, it will require you to rebuild yourself. It is only in the rebuilding of your thoughts, that you will help to stop your child from enduring similar situations such as yours. Otherwise, if you don't heal mentally, spiritually, and emotionally you will teach those same behaviors to your child who will then repeat the same cycle.

We have a duty as a parent to give our children more than we were given. Each generation is smarter than the last. So, although you may be like me and may not have gotten that sense of safety and security that you yearned for or needed as a child, you owe it to your child to give it to them!

If you can get your children professional help, you should also be talking with your child. Ask their thoughts, opinions, gauge, and understand their feelings. Doing so will help you to gain the strength to leave the situation, but it will also help your child to know that someone cares about how they feel in addition to getting them to verbalize their emotions to avoid them internalizing their thoughts and emotions. Doing this is imperative because it also helps your child to know that the behavior in which they have witnessed or heard is not normal, but if you don't point it out to them as they become older they begin to seek out what seems to be 'familiar to them and unintentionally they begin to repeat the cycle of abuse.

Also, commend children on things they do well. Discuss academic milestones. Find out your child's interests and dislikes and focus on cultivating those things so that your child can be the best version of themselves unapologetically. Get in a habit of celebrating their achievements, so that they too will celebrate their achievements in life and leave less room for the enemy within to sabotage and or discredit their success as they come along in life.

Teach your child about self-affirmations. Affirmations are words of emotional support or encouragement. When a child is taught from birth who they are and they believe those words they are less likely to be persuaded by the world, peer pressure, or become beat down by various situations. Hearing that they are smart, strong, beautiful, accomplished, successful, etc. gets down into their subconscious and they begin to believe that they are those things and so they grow up acting like they have been listening to.

My last tip would be that as you read this book if you don't already, get a living will drawn up in which you outline your wishes on where you want your child to be raised and by whom. Make sure that person will be someone who will carry out your wishes with your children in the same way as you would and also state your wishes on how you would like your insurance policy to be spent. For example, if $50,000 is to be set aside for your child to go to college then state that in your will. If you are not careful, insurance money you leave for your child/ren can be used on other people and items that are not for the benefit of your children. Be intentional about how you live your life, but also prepare for when you are no longer on earth.

Reckless: Fury of being Scorn

If a problem is not fixed at the root, it will continue to surface in various situations in your life until you recognize the issue and work to fix it at the root. Translation, if you recognize a familiar situation in your life that keeps reoccurring; it is not the people around you. It is something within yourself that is causing you to attract those exterior situations, relationships, people, etc. It is the law of Cause and Effect.

We attract what we are. Nothing happens by chance outside of the universal law. The law of relativity teaches us that each person receives their share of challenges/tests with the purpose of strengthening the light within. We must consider each of these tests as an opportunity.

For change to occur, it first starts internally. For God to grow you into the person in which you were created to be, there must be a series of testing your heart throughout your life, so that things like pride, arrogance, and selfishness can be worked out of you. If you trust the process you will come to find the beauty in life as things begin to work for you and come to you with ease and little effort.

Life is meant to be a beautiful experience even with the challenges. However, we have been conditioned to look at the challenges as a negative experience rather than seeing the lessons in them and growing from them.

Each of us has a story and just as I am telling my story to you to help encourage and guide you; you have a story as well that is meant to help and guide someone else. The key to life is perseverance and resiliency. If you can master those two things nothing in life can or will conquer you.

****

I had enough of my psycho ex-boyfriend, and I wanted out of the relationship; however, every time, I got ready to break up with him, he became Romeo and I mean literally. He would express his deep-rooted love for me and tell me how if I did not want to be with him then he would kill himself. Hook line and sinker for me with the guilt. I did not want to wake up one day and see it on the news that he had killed himself because I wanted to break up with him. So, what did I do? I stayed.

At this point in my life, I did not recognize that this too was another form of abuse/manipulation. Again, as I stated earlier, abuse is not always physical it can also be mental.

In 2003, a year after graduating from high school, I met a guy who was out of my comfort zone. He was older, shorter, had a stockier build, as opposed to the younger athletic build type of guys I had been used to dating. He had a nice SUV with rims on it and a loud sound system. In the collegiate world that I find myself in today, he could have been considered a 'thug', a 'gangster', or a 'drug dealer'. However, back in those days and in my neighborhood, he was a 'Baller' a guy who had street creditability and money to spend. I will not disclose the Baller's actual name but will keep his identity to myself and just refer to him going forward as 'Baller'.

At that time when Baller came into my life, I had dated small-time 'thugs'/wannabes, but not a guy of his caliber. So, I did not even take him seriously that he liked me. Many females in my neighborhood, would have been throwing themselves at him, in fact, they were. Growing up in the ghetto and coming from a household of having just enough, being with a "baller" was like being with a guy from the NBA. Most girls wanted to find a 'Baller', and have kids with him so that she could be financially taken care of by him. Translation: Use his kids against him for her financial gain.

Personally, I was not impressed by his money, cars, or jewelry because honestly, I did not even know until I moved out of the ghetto that I was living in the ghetto. I did not know until I got older and started working in Corporate America that I had grown up impoverished. I had a roof over my head, cable to watch, I was warm in the winter, had food on the table every night, and I had a family who loved me dearly. I did not realize that we sometimes slept on cots in our dining room in front of the Kerosene heater, due to our gas being shut off. I did not realize that it was not normal to hear gunshots every night. My grandmother and I would sit on the couch and watch TV. with the front and backdoors open until 11 pm and not flinch as we heard gunshots ring out. Yet, I thought this was normal, so no I was not impressed by this Baller.

I had not told my current boyfriend that I met someone else, but he found out one day as he was down the street and saw me get out of the Baller's truck. Oh, hell has no fury like a man scorn. That saying does not only apply to women. When he found out

I soon learned just how psycho he really could be. I mean we are talking breaking into my grandparent's home and crawling on the floor for me to open my eyes and find him beside me on the floor or following me while I was out with the Baller.

One night, as I was getting dropped off, he followed the Baller and I to my house, and as soon as I got into the house he was on the front porch. As I was on the phone trying to call the police, the next thing I know he kicked in the front door, hit me in the head with something, and then ran out the back door. I filed charges but never went through with the full prosecution to have him convicted and sent to prison. That is me.

No matter how much a person does to me, I find myself not wishing or wanting the worse for them. I now know that it is called forgiveness. I also know that God lives within us, and so we also have his same characteristics, which include love and forgiveness. So, sometimes even if we want to be mad or upset with someone, we find ourselves forgiving them and wanting to move on.

Now, you know that it is the inner source within you allowing you to forgive the person so that you can move on freely with life. For some people forgiveness is something they truly struggle with in their lives; however, it has always come extremely easy to me. The downside is that it has also gotten me into some bad situations because I tend to forgive and then try to re-establish the relationship with the person and they end up manipulating my forgiveness as a weakness and sometime it has caused me to end up right back in another bad situation. As much as I did not want to forgive some people in my life, there was always something on the inside of me that would forgive them, but not forget. I believe if you forget, you are susceptible to it occurring again; however, in forgiving you are not to continue to throw it up in the person's face repeatedly.

Once you have forgiven the person you move on. Some people may say, 'She's dumb', or 'She's such a pushover', you may be saying it right now as you are reading these stories. I know people say those things because I heard them all while going through my situation. However, in the midst of people judging what I really could have used were some kind words or another woman who had been through domestic violence to wrap her arms around me and share her story, encourage me, and let me know that she survived and I would too!

So, after filing charges against my psycho now ex-boyfriend he was out of the picture for a while and I began to spend more time with the Baller, whom I discovered was fourteen years older than me. The age difference at first had me a little disgusted because I thought he was only eight years older than me. I was always the one telling my friends why they should not date older men because what does an older man have in common with us? He probably only wants one thing… SEX! So, I assumed that was all he wanted as well, and that once he got it, he would be gone. It is so funny, as we spiritual beings having this human experience for the first time, we think that the things that we are or have experienced are new to us, but the truth is that they are not.

History repeats itself and the situations are made relevant for its time. So, although I was disgusted with the age difference between us, I thought of my grandparents who were also fourteen years apart, as well as many of the couples in the Bible. I did not allow the age difference to get in the way of seeing where this new relationship would take me.

I recall one day being with him and he had bought me a couple of these dresses that were in style at the time called "jersey dresses". If your unfamiliar with them Google them ☺. I was trying them on and showing him how they looked, and he commented to one of his friends "Yeah, she's mine. I am locking her down for life". I laughed and in the back of my mind, I was wondering what I had got myself into. Have I just potentially got myself into another relationship with another psycho?

Several months went by and one day as we are spending time together the Baller says to me "I think I am falling in love with you". I honestly, did not feel the same way. I felt after three months of knowing each other it was impossible to love someone, so how do you love me? I may have said something to the effects of "But you don't even know me". He replied, "I know that I am falling in love with you".

Again, relating this moment to Biblical times, God created Adam first, and then he created Eve for Adam as a helpmate. In saying this, I believe that men are to find themselves a wife and that they know when they have found the one. The Bible says, "Blessed is a man who finds himself a wife". So, the Baller's feelings at that time may have been very genuine. I think that by me not telling him that I felt the same way about him made him feel insecure about me and our relationship because he would ask me if I loved him and why I loved him.

At first, I would answer and probably with some not so great answers because it takes me a while to love, but when I do, I love HARD. I was guarded when it came to falling in love with men, due to not having my father's love. They say that is the first man a little girl falls in love with and the reason why many women who grow up having their fathers in their lives are less likely to lower themselves to the standards of mental and physical abuse from a man unless her father also mentally and physically abused her or her mother.

So, getting back to the Baller and him asking me why I loved him, he asked me this question one day and I replied, "If you have to ask if I love you and why then you must not feel like I do, so then you may want to figure out why you're even with me." I was really getting irritated with him asking this question repeatedly.

Well, just like the last relationship he too became possessive. He purchased me a cellphone and I was excited but did not realize it was only to track what I was doing and where I was. See, here is the thing about dating a street "Baller". The money is nice. Really nice. It is nice to have whatever you want when you want it; without waiting on a paycheck. However, it also comes with a high price tag and I was not ready to pay the price in which I would soon be faced to pay.

Many guys, who are out in the streets making 'fast' money, typically do not have a strong religious foundation. The Bible says that you cannot serve two Gods because you will love the one and hate the other. Therefore, you cannot serve God and Money. I say this to say, due to the Baller having such a love for Money, it became his God and therefore, his soul was dark!

One evening while lying in the bed we had a disagreement about something I do not recall what it was exactly, but I went and got into the bed in the other room. The next thing I knew he came into the room and played a voicemail of a guy I had met before dating him and the guy never called me by name he always addressed me as 'Baby', probably because he had so many other females he didn't want to get us mixed up or he never took the time to learn my name. So, on the voicemail, the guy says, "Hey Baby…". The Baller then proceeds to ask who it was and I am telling him it was a guy that I met before him and the next thing I know he takes his thumb and gouges it into my eye, so hard that the blood vessels in my eye popped. He begins to call me some explicit names and we somehow end up in my bedroom. He takes his belt, ties it around my neck, and then hangs me from the closet door. Talk about humiliating. I think I was more hurt because after all the things that I endured with my ex; I trusted the Baller. He knew the things that I had gone through and yet he proved to be no different.

I kept asking myself how I got into that place. How do you go from one domestic violence relationship into another before the age of 21? What I did not know back then is that the abuse that I observed as a child made me susceptible to the comfort of abuse. It felt familiar to me and for that reason, I did what I saw my mother do growing up and I stayed in the relationship. I brushed it underneath the rug as if it never happened, lied to family, friends, and co-workers about what had happened to my eye.

The Baller feeling guilty for his actions was comforting and buying me gifts. As odd as it might sound, I began to become accustomed to the attention that I received after a fight or argument. It made me feel wanted, needed and appreciated. However, this was a sign of untreated trauma that probably stemmed back from my childhood days. My brain was now under the impression that the abuse hurt, but afterward, you just forget about it and you and the abuser will makeup and things will go back to normal.

From the early childhood trauma that I witnessed to the two domestic violence relationships that I found myself in, my brain was no longer functioning how it was designed. I guess you can say that it was offline and until I sought professional help when I was ready, I would continue to make decisions that would put my safety and life at risk.

****

After that situation with the Baller, I had gotten back in touch with my ex. Yes, my ex as in my 'psycho ex-boyfriend'. The Baller ended up being placed into a work-release program for a conviction he had before meeting me. So, he was allowed out to go to work around 7 am and had to be back around 6 or 7 pm each evening.

22

I had quit my job and the Baller was paying my rent, bills, and even bought me a car. I was in school full time. When the Baller went into the work release center at night, I began to allow my ex to come back around. The Bible says that **the enemy comes seeking, to kill, steal, and destroy whom he may devour.** By enemy, I do not mean a red demon with horns. When I speak of the enemy throughout this book, I am referring to the 'Inner Me'. Enemy is a play on words to mean In Me or Inner Me. I was getting ready to find out exactly what was meant by that scripture.

My ex and I started out with talks down memory lane on the phone, which eventually led to him coming over, which ended with us becoming sexually involved. The Bible also says t**he spirit is willing, but the flesh is weak.** I knew what I was doing was wrong. I was in a committed relationship; however, I was still having sex with my ex. I guess you can say I was having the best of both worlds, but not really because I was getting ready to experience hell on earth.

See, if you allow your inner self or your enemy within an inch, you will soon find yourself going a mile. Who knows you better than you? Your wants and desires even i those wants and desires are not good for us, it doesn't mean we don't desire to have them or partake in them, but we have to have knowledge, wisdom, and self-control to guard ourselves from those things.

The 20-year-old me did not realize that being sexually involved with my ex gave him hope that there was still a chance for us to be together. I personally was just in it for the pleasure and had no hopes of us getting back together.

I also underestimated the feelings that the Baller had for me and just how hot his temper could run. Playing with the emotions of both individuals was getting ready to become a dangerous recipe for disaster for me.

I am not sure how the Baller found out, but eventually, everything caught up to me. The Baller ended up finding out that I was still sneaking around with my ex and the day he confronted me I did not think I would be living to tell this story to you today.

****

It was the late spring of 2004. I was getting ready for class. I got a phone call from the Baller and he told me not to drive my car and that he was on his way. Okay, I thought. He came into the house, in a fit of rage and he kept asking me was I still messing around with my ex. I was 120 lbs back then and he was close to 300 lbs. So, out of fear I said no. The next thing I knew he grabbed me by my corn rolls that I had in my hair and dragged me up the stairs. As I was being dragged up the stairs my corn rolls are literally being detached from my scalp from him pulling me so hard by my hair. Once into my bedroom, while I am on the floor, he proceeds to ask me again if I had been messing around with my ex. I said no. The next several hours consisted of a brutal beating of him punching me and kicking me. At one point I was almost unconscious, and I recall him saying "Wake up bitch. You not about to die on me yet" and he slapped me across my face. He was so upset; I recall him taking the iron off my dresser and turning it on high. He then puts it close to my face and says "Yeah, I'm about to mess your pretty face all up". I took my hand to try and protect my face and ended up hitting the iron with my hand, which ended up leaving a second-degree burn. I still have the scar on my left hand to remind me to this day.

In addition to the beating, he took the time to have his way with me, vaginally and anally. As he was doing so, he gripped his hands tightly around my neck, and says "I wonder what the pussy feels like when you're dead".

He then tells me to go into the closet and he takes nails and a hammer and nails the closet door shut. He then says, "We're about to do an experiment and see how long you can last without food and water".

I remember praying and asking God to forgive me of my sins because I thought that I was going to die. I had two black eyes, my nose was bleeding, my face was swollen, my hair that was once intertwined with weave was now detached from my scalp on the right side of my head leaving me with a bald patch and not to mention my body was aching from the multiple punches to my body I had received. My body was tired. I had been getting beat up for at least four or five hours straight no breaks in between.

Amid being in the closet one of my friends called and he told her I was not home. He then calls one of his children's mothers and tells her how he wanted to see her and that he loved her. I guess to make me jealous. He ended up leaving and the irony in him leaving was that he left to go check in with his probation officer. I thought when you were on probation you were supposed to stay out of trouble and here, he had just almost committed murder and goes to check in with his probation officer.

While he was gone, I began banging on the wall in the closet to see if I could make a hole big enough to crawl through (call it survival instincts or too many Lifetime movies with my grandmother).

Behind my closet was the bathroom sink. So, I figured if I could make a hole big enough, I could escape. I was not able to get the task accomplished in time. He arrived back and eventually, he opened the closet and let me out.

When I got out of the closet the Maury Povich show was on, which typically came on back in that day around 4 pm. Between the beating and me being locked in the closet it was literally an all-day event. From 8 am until 4 pm.

After releasing me from the closet he told me to get into the bed and he gave me some pills to take. I asked him what they were, and he just told me to take them. Out of fear I did not question him. As he lay at the head of the bed and I was at the foot, I remember climbing up to the head of the bed and asking if I could lie on his chest. I laid down and whatever, those pills were they knocked me out.

When I woke up, he was gone, and it was the next day. I awoke to the phone ringing. It was him saying that he was going to go to Boston Market and get something to eat and asked if I wanted something. I said yes. The tone in his voice was as if everything that took place yesterday never had happened. After I got off the phone, I realized that he was gone.

I was so scared of him coming back, I got up, got dressed, got into my car, and drove over to one of my cousin's houses. When I arrived, I told her everything that had happened, but by the look on my face that showed I had been brutally beaten, she knew something had taken place. She asked what I wanted to do, and I said that I wanted to go press charges. I wanted him to go to jail for what he had done to me. I was also scared that he would come back and do something else to me. I was afraid that the next time he beat me up, I would not survive.

We drove downtown and upon speaking with someone and telling them my story, they told me to go over to the hospital so that a rape kit could be performed and that a detective would meet me over at the hospital. We got to the hospital sometime around maybe 11 am or 12 pm. The nurse asked several questions, and then took me into a room and performed a rape kit on me, which involves them taking specimen from the vaginal area, pictures with a high tech piece of equipment that could show the rips and tears in the vaginal and anus areas. They then proceeded to take pictures of all my bruises, which seemed to be all over my body, from head to toe. As she was finishing up, a detective came in to get my story of what had taken place that day.

After finishing up at close to 11 pm, I walked out of the room and literally, my aunts, cousins, and some other people were in the waiting room. Talk about embarrassed. I gave my cousin the dirtiest look. I confided in her and she had my whole family at the emergency room. Here I was with my face looking distorted and bruises all over my body. I did not want to be seen by anyone. She said it was not her fault that they were all there. She said she told one person and you know how that goes, you tell one, they tell one, and then they tell one and the next thing you know everyone knows.

I arrived at my house and was met by the detective. He asked if I had heard from the Baller. I said no. Upon entering my house, I discovered that the Baller had brought back my cellphone and laid it on the couch. I grabbed it and as I was outside with my family, friends, and the detective my phone rings. I look up at the detective and say, "it's him". He says answer it and act normal.

As I was on the phone the detective asked for my family and friends to disperse. I lived in a half a double at the time. So, I sat on my back porch and the detective on the other side of the duplex. I asked the Baller was he coming over and he said, "no". Then he asked me where I had been. He said he went to Boston Market and when he got to my house I was gone. I said, "I was at my cousin's house". He then says, "who is that sitting outside with you"? I said, "I don't know, somebody at the neighbor's house. Where are you"? As I am talking the detective is speaking to officers over his radio.

The next thing I know undercover cars were swooping in from all directions, then the marked police cars arrived to block in the Baller. I had no clue that the whole time, my street was full of undercover cops. I felt like the president with the secret service.

The next thing, I knew they had gotten the Baller out of his car and arrested him. I was a little shaken up and went to stay at my cousin's apartment for the night. I remember her talking to me and that is when she began to share stories with me about domestic violence situations she had endured in her earlier years. She said, "you will know when you have had enough, and when you do, you'll leave. Until that point, there is nothing anyone can tell you to get you to leave".

It took me several years to get that revelation, but when I did my life changed forever!

Depend on the Lord for strength.
Always go to him for help
~ 1 Chronicles 16:11

Restored: From Fury and Being Scorned

Wow!! This chapter of my life was one of the hardest and most difficult times I had endured. The biggest mistake that I made in my relationship with the Baller was staying after the eye gouging incident, which was the first time he put his hands on me. Mya Angelou said it best "If someone shows you who they are BELIEVE them". When the Baller gouged my eyeball there should have never been a second chance with him. By not leaving him, I allowed the Baller to believe that I would stay with him no matter what, there would be no reprimand for his actions, and I had no family to come to my rescue.

Growing up I did not have anyone reinforcing the fact that I was a princess who would grow up to be a beautiful queen and worthy of nothing less than respect. So, if no one has ever told you this I am telling you right now YOU ARE A BEAUTIFUL PRINCESS or QUEEN. You are worthy and valuable, and no one has the right to ever disrespect you whether that is verbal or non-verbal.

If you don't tell the world how to treat you, then you give permission for people to treat you however they may feel. Don't allow others to determine your worth. The right people will see your value and will cherish your thoughts, feelings/emotions, and your well being. Allow your emotions to be your guide. Our inner being is always with us and trying to guide us to what is rightfully ours and wants us to experience an abundantly great and happy life. If you give a person, the smallest inclination that you will settle for disrespect the person will use it as control, and the abuse will only escalate. No one has the right to reduce your value or worth in this world to less than what you were created to be in this world. If domestic violence occurs once, cut your losses, and walk away. It does not get better. The incidents only get worse. Each time that you're involved in a domestic violence situation, you are playing rush and roulette with your life because you aren't guaranteed to walk away from those situations, and each time, you're getting closer and closer to death.

I also learned accountability from this situation. You cannot play with the hearts and minds of others because you never know how they handle those situations. Not only that it's just not cool to cheat on others. Do unto others as you would want others to do unto you. It may not always be a good idea to jump out of one relationship and straight into the next one without first taking some time to heal yourself from the previous relationship.

If I had the chance to do life over again, I would have gone to counseling, journaled, prayed, meditated after leaving my ex-boyfriend. Perhaps, if I had done that, I would have had more clarity when choosing my next spouse. If I had gone to counseling, I would have understood that since I had been exposed to domestic violence as a child, I subconsciously was seeking a spouse who seemed 'familiar'. I would have been able to make the connection early on between being exposed to domestic violence and experiencing domestic violence and I could have prevented being in a violent relationship with the Baller. However, since I did not take time to heal, I ended up attracting the very thing in which I did not want to be around. The energy of the Baller was familiar and familiar is not always a good place to be, especially if familiar brought about hurt and pain to your life. However, that is why counseling is imperative because it helps you to recognize where the familiarity arose from and how you ended up gravitating towards it into your adulthood. However, if you do not recognize the familiar pattern in your life you will continue to attract the very energy in which you know you do not want nor deserve. Often in life, it is okay to be uncomfortable.

As humans, we always want to strive for comfort, but the growth is in being uncomfortable. Healing the mind, body, and soul, is a daily process. It never stops. Once you decide to enter into a new relationship, there will be things that trigger you from past relationships, especially if you are still healing from the inside out. The important part is that you notice those triggers and you self-reflect on them and find some sort of way to process those feelings whether it be through meditation, writing, dancing, etc., embrace those emotions, bless them, and let it go. When we bless the situation that did not mean us any good in our lives we transform the energy. So, for instance I may say, "I bless the domestic violence relationship that I endured and anticipate a healthy, vibrant, and loving relationship to find me. I am giving off loving and healthy energies to attract what I deserve". I am now releasing my past and making room for my future to find me.

When you meditate, think about how it would feel to be in the arms of a loving spouse that you can talk to openly and without fears. Think about how you want your life to be and feel all of the emotions that arise from those beautiful thoughts. I guarantee you, if you can do this and free yourself from your past you will attract into your life the very thing you deserve and that method works for anything not just relationships.

My last tip is that as you move forth in life and seek out a new mate, be mindful and aware of what the person says, watch their actions, watch how they treat other women in their life (mother, daughter, sister, etc), a person can only pretend to be a representative for so long before the real them appears.

Recklessly Losing Pieces of My Soul

After the incident that took place on May 25, 2004; I knew of God but realized I did not have a relationship with my inner being. The God that lives on the inside of me. It was not until later in life that I discovered that God is energy and he created us in his image, making us a divine god creation as well. Ultimately, meaning God dwells in each of us. We are God manifested in the earth in human form. So, if we are spiritually divine beings trying to navigate this human experience on earth why is it, we disregard our true divine selves and settle for the obscurities of what we have become accustomed to on earth? Who introduced us to mediocrity? I am sure you have dreams and aspirations for your life, correct? God placed those inside of you and he will lead you like a GPS to get them out of you and into this earthly realm.

Do you have dreams while you asleep or stare off while awake and daydream about certain things? Those moments once again are God trying to give you a glimpse of your future and guide you into your purpose.

The law of Divine Oneness states that all energy is an extension of source energy. We are all energy connected to source energy, which is God. God wants us to tap into the divine power in which we are an extension and unlock our inner potential, but only a select few of us ever do. In the Bible, there is a verse that says, "many are called, but only few are chosen". There are only a select few people who will do the work to tap into their god divine power in which they were born equipped, simply because they believe the lies of this world which feed their inner me or enemy on a daily basis causing them to believe that they are not worthy and lack power over themselves and their situations. All the situations and circumstances that happen in our lives are preparation for our destiny.

I used to believe that the 13 years of single parenting I endured was due to God preparing me for my destiny. However, I now realize that it was simply the law of cause and effect. I attracted the Baller into my life due to what I had been exposed to and what I had been raised around. I had no idea that the trauma and dysfunction that I endured was not only in my psyche, but it was in my vibrational aura. That energy was being given off and I attracted the very thing in which I thought I would never deal with in a relationship.

The cause and effect behind that decision was that I ended up raising a child alone for 13 years and repeated the cycle of domestic violence. My dependence on the Baller financially and my lack of financial education from my family caused me to endure some hard and painful times as a woman and as a mother.

In 2008, it was as if in the spiritual realm, God said that it was 'time'. It was time to start building me into the person which I was created to become, to start reaching the people whom I was destined to touch, and for me to leave a glimmer of hope on the inside of those people.

I did not know that the incident that had transpired on May 25, 2004, would be the catalyst God would use to begin the starting point of my life's transformation. We sometimes think back on our lives and wish that we had done some things differently; however, it is those things that build our character. It is the pain we endure that teaches us to have empathy and compassion for others. It is the lessons that we endure and learn from that allow us to bestow our knowledge onto others who may be faced with that same situation, so I no longer think back and wish I did things differently because it was those things that built me into the woman that I am today.

****

The Baller was now sitting in the county jail, with a severely high bond. I did not realize back then, but I now know that the Baller had some unresolved traumas that ran deep. They were buried down so deep that he was unaware of them, but they were showing themselves in how he treated the women in his life. Anger is a secondary emotion that never comes alone. Typically, where you find anger you find vulnerable emotions. However, the Baller was not going to allow anyone to get close enough to him to discover what those vulnerable emotions were because he took that as a sign of weakness, which many men in our society do, particularly black men. Society has made black men feel as if being vulnerable is a sign that they are not 'Real Men'. Now, we have men walking around with pent up emotions that run as far back as to their ancestors being raped, beaten, and sold on plantation fields.

The Baller was not the only one dealing with unresolved trauma. I was as well. I kept packing on the trauma without ever addressing the issues that occurred in my childhood. In turn, I developed a running away mentality. I ran away from issues because it allowed me to escape the pain. So, due to running away from my issues, it allowed me to stay in that psychological mind frame of thinking everything was okay. That is why when the Baller would call me from the county jail and say things like "it' just us and we are in this together, or we are going to get through this I believed him"

What I didn't realize was that the fact that I had witnessed domestic violence as a child, been in one domestic violence relationship, and now had let it occur again, was probably a sign that I should also seek help. Not to mention, the fact that I was a daddy less daughter. That is a whole other book. What part of allowing a man to pound on you was normal? What part of not valuing myself as a black queen did, I no understand? What part of God being within me, so that made me royalty was I not understanding? As small as it seems these are the slight variations in the difference between a woman growing up with a father and one growing up without one. When a little girl grows up with her father in her life her dad is constantly treating her as his princess. That little girl means the world to that man and he is willing to go toe to toe with anyone who hurts his princess. A father is the first man that a little girl falls in love with in her life. However, when you grow up without having a father in your life as a child, you subconsciously seek out that father figure in men you date.

We as women were created as helpmates to men, so deep down inside it is instinctive that we want or need to have male companionship beginning as a youth. Our fathers are supposed to show us and guide us as to what the characteristics are of a good man so that we know what to look for in a mate. However, if you did not grow up having that example in your life, then unfortunately you will seek out what is familiar in your relationships based on your environmental or societal influences on your psyche growing up. This is not something that is done consciously, but that is done subconsciously. For example, if you were never taught to close your mouth while eating food, then you probably as an adult still chew your food with your mouth open. You do not realize what you are doing until someone else points it out because it is something that you do subconsciously. The same holds true for daddy less daughters, when they choose the men they date they don't say to themselves I want to find a deadbeat like my father, but many times they end up choosing men who are abusers, aggressors, liars, cheaters, men who abandon them, are promiscuous, etc.

They say you do not miss what you never had and that saying is so far from the truth. We share 50% of our parent's DNA, so you are your mother and father. So, despite not having one or both in your life you yearn for that relationship to be fulfilled in your life. So, therefore Daddy less daughters end up falling for men who are wolves in sheep's clothing portraying to be her knight in shining armor. These men prey on women by lying to them. They say they will provide for them and protect them and never hurt or abandon them. I guess they are partially telling the truth because they do provide and protect, but at a price.

Although I had my grandfather and uncles in my life, I was still a daddy less daughter. In my case, I was an orphan, Daddy less, and motherless. I excelled academically in school, but streetwise, I was lost and trying to find my way, which led me to being abused physically and mentally. Which is how I ended up in relationships such as the one with my ex as well as the Baller, who at this time had spent a couple of months in the county jail before his friends were able to help him liquidate some assets and raise his bond. In the midst, he coached me telling me that if I did not go to court or cooperate, then the case would be dropped and go away. He told me that if he were convicted, he could be facing 20-30 years.

I knew he had children and I did not want him to go away that long and miss out on being a parent to his children and believe it or not, I still had feelings for him. So, upon his release, things appeared to be going back to normal.

My lease was up at my place and I found another one in a better neighborhood. The Baller paid my first month's rent and deposit, as well as arranged to have him and his friends to help me move and although I would have liked to think that he did this because he cared about my wellbeing, he was only pushing to help me move so that when the subpoenas started to show up for me to go to court, the prosecutors would no longer have a physical address for their witness.

What I thought was love was just another game of manipulation and control. Upon moving into my new place, I thought that this would be a fresh start for our relationship. I thought that after all we had gone through, we would put it all behind us and start rebuilding our relationship. However, it was the loneliest time ever. The Baller was not coming around as much, he was not answering his phone for me as much, we stopped spending time together like we used to when we first met. He was still holding a grudge against me for sleeping around with my ex-boyfriend. He also began to cheat on me. I began to get phone calls where someone would call and hang up when I answered. One day the girl finally decided to say something when I answered the phone and she told me her name and that she had been messing around with the Baller. He denied it, but after that incident took place, I became suspicious and I began to do a little more snooping on my own. The girl would call his cellphone at 5 am and 6 am and he would tell me that it was his male friend because of course, he didn't have her actual name saved on his phone. All the females on his phone were stored as nicknames. At least this is what I discovered after snooping through his phone. I would then find pictures that he took with the mother of one of his children and he would deny it being anything relational, outside of pictures he took while spending time with his child.

Although, I knew he was lying to me. I still stayed, but then I began to seek attention from other places. I began turning to the internet and talking to guys online. One online relationship moved from being online to us being on the phone every day all day. The Baller found out and appeared to be hurt but then hurt turned into anger. He eventually stopped paying my rent causing me to get evicted. The irony in him no longer paying my rent was that he did it after the case between the two of us had been tossed out due to the star witness (me) not being available to testify.

After being evicted I went and stayed with my uncle for about a month or so. In that period of my life, I felt hurt, abandoned, and used. I felt that had I showed up to court perhaps he would still be around me and acted like he cared for me. Do you see my rationale in thinking at that point in my life? These were clear obvious signs of trauma. When someone experiences trauma the brain is unable to process rational thinking. It is as if it goes offline and once you heal you can choose to stay broken and the victim, the same person you once were, or you can emerge a stronger, more resilient version of yourself.

Right, before I got evicted, I had gotten a job working as a canvasser for a local basement finishing company. My job was to go around and knock on doors and try to get the homeowner to set an appointment for an estimate. If the homeowner, set up an appointment and allowed the salesmen to come out I received a $50 commission on top of my $8/hr.

Being able to stay with my uncle I was able to save up enough money to get my own apartment. By the grace of God, the eviction was not showing up on my credit report and I was able to obtain approval on a little one-bedroom apartment. It was such a great feeling. I was able to get an apartment all on my own without the help of the Baller. This man had been paying all my bills and rent for the last three years. By being able to pay my own bills, I was now gaining back control over my life.

The Baller helped me to move into my new place but soon began to get an attitude because I did not give him a key. Why should he get a key? He did not even help me to obtain the apartment. He was the reason I had gotten evicted.

Things were still rocky with our relationship. I felt alone and abandoned. I got tired of telling him how I felt and him not changing his behavior. I got tired of crying and feeling hurt due to finding text messages and pictures from other women.

After getting fed up, I decided to 'Do Me'. Meaning, if he wanted to see other women, then I would see other men. I became physically reckless to myself. My morals and values were tossed by the wayside because I no longer wanted to feel hurt. I wanted to feel wanted and needed even if it meant just in the moment. In that phase of my life, I was not able to hear God and I was not looking to spend time with him. I did.not know or care about myself. I was looking for my worth to be determined by a man and that cost me pain, sanity, and the loss of my dignity. All I knew was that I was lonely and in need of love or at least that is what my inner me aka enemy (in me) allowed me to believe.

I was trying to fill the void of feeling abandoned. My father abandoned me, my mother passed away, and I had lost my grandfather. My support system was gone and there was a pain on the inside that I thought being in a relationship with a man could/would fill for me. The inner me believed that if I wanted to keep a man that sleeping with him was the way to go and that if I did not sleep with him, he would not want to stay with me. God created sex to be a beautiful bond shared between men and women… yes. However, it was meant to be between two committed people who are married. The act of sex is what joins the two as one and allows them to procreate and multiply the earth. This is God's perfect plan of the family structure (Man, Woman, Children). However, your enemy likes to destroy and distort everything that God designed as perfect by planting seeds of deception. So, when you're unwed and having sex with multiple people you begin to intertwine your soul with multiple people and their soul intertwines with yours as well. Once this occurs you begin to carry the energy of these different people making it rather hard to focus on yourself, find your purpose in this world, and heal from past hurts.

****

My dad was absent in my life, the Baller was no longer showing he cared for me, so my quest for love began or I should say my quest for what I thought was love.

I was on the bus one day and I met this guy. He was cute and funny. Before the end of the bus ride, we exchanged phone numbers. Our phone conversations eventually led to him coming over to my house and us becoming sexually involved with each other. I thought he was cool, but I soon became bored by the fact that every time I called him, he was never at home. He would then pop up to my apartment unannounced and expecting to have sex with me. I realized that this was not something that I wished to entertain any longer and so one day as he was calling my phone, I kept sending him to voicemail. The next thing I knew I had a knock on the door, and it was him asking why I was not answering my phone. I nonchalantly told him that I was in the middle of working out. He proceeds to say 'so, you couldn't answer your phone?' I replied, "no. I couldn't. I am busy". He then asks if he could come in and I told him no. He looks at me like a lost puppy and I ask him if he needs anything else because I would like to return to my work out. He says, "so, you're really not going to let me in". "Uh, no". I could see the conversation was not getting anywhere so; I politely closed the door and continued with my workout. I know it probably was not the nicest thing to do. I was around 21 or 22 at the time and if you asked people who knew me, they would say that is because I was mean. I did not find it mean; I just do not like to waste my time. So, that was the end of that short-lived romance.

So, I am sure you are wondering about the Baller. Yes, he was still in the picture at this point. He was still on the streets a lot because that is how he made his money, but he was beginning to show me more attention like he used to do. He was coming around a little more and we would go out on his motorcycle for bike rides, out for dinner, etc. It was as if he subconsciously had a feeling that he was slowly losing me and decided to try and pay more attention to me to try and hang on to our relationship. However, I did not trust him, and therefore, I continued to 'Do Me'.

The Baller had gotten me a laptop. So, being young and bored I began surfing the internet and at that time we had a couple of websites called "Black Planet" and "My Space". There was also a dating website called match.com. I had profiles on all of them and I was talking to various people.

I ended up meeting one guy on match.com and we spoke on the phone a couple of times before I let him come over. After exchanging conversations, I soon discovered that this guy rode motorcycles with the same circle of friends as the Baller. So, I asked if he knew the Baller and come to find out he did. He informed me that they were acquaintances, but not super tight, so we were cool and if I did not say anything neither would he.

Ladies, saints, and gents do not judge me, but I became sexually involved with him as well. Unprotected!! Come to find out he lived at home with his daughter and her mother.

The Baller being back up to his old tricks began to get suspicious and somehow or another discovered that I had been talking to guys online. He was rather upset that I had been doing it on the laptop that he gave to me. So, of course, he takes the laptop back. He somehow also discovered that I had been talking to his motorcycle counterpart.

So, one day as they are all hanging out, I get a phone call from the Baller, not knowing that he was with his motorcycle counterpart and that they had been exchanging information. I became so angry with his motorcycle counterpart, not only was he potentially putting himself at risk of a brutal beating, but me as well by telling him that we had been involved and to the depths at which we had been involved. So, I began to tell the Baller how this guy told me that the Baller was living with his baby mom and how he had been to the house and seen the Ballers bikes over there and the girl as well and he knows for a fact that is where he lived. It did not make me mad finding out the information because I suspected it. I confronted the Baller about it, and he would lie and say that he did not live with her. I found out this information a couple of years earlier when I found the title to one of his vehicles in his car and I saw the girls name and address on the title. The fact that his motorcycle counterpart had told me this piece of information, made the Baller furious and at this point he was ready to beat the crap out of this guy. I am laughing in the meantime because this guy must have thought I was just some sort of cheap thrill and thought that it would be okay to brag about me to the Baller, not knowing the depths of him and I's relationship and the fact that the Baller had really strong feelings for me. So, I figured since he was that dumb to do such a thing then he deserved the repercussions of his actions.

So, the Baller began to get a dose of his own medicine, and let us just say he did not like it. Things seemed cool between us for a little while. He was back around and spending more time with me and our life seemed to be normal.

I had made up my mind that I wanted to have a baby. In early 2007, I told the Baller that I wanted a baby and that I was determined to have one whether it was with him or not. In fact, I was so determined to have a baby that I had unprotected sex with the short-term bus romance, the Ballers motorcycle counterpart, as well as with the Baller. Do not judge me ya'll. This was the 22-year-old me, young and reckless.

This was a behavior that I had never engaged in; however, hurt and pain can push you to be at a level of low in which you have never been. I was tired of the Baller lying to me saying he loved me, he wanted to be with me, and yet he would leave my house and go and be with other females.

In my pursuit to get pregnant, the Baller and I went to see a fertility specialist. She asked us several questions and after determining there wasn't anything wrong with the Baller's sperm count due to him having 11 other kids, she scheduled to have me go and take a test in which we could see rather or not my tubes were scarred.

Yes, the Baller has 11 children. When I found this piece of news out it was too late I had already begun to have feelings for him. Had I known this in the very beginning I probably would have run the other way. Especially, since he has them by nine different women.

Another reason I did not leave when he told me was because I did not care. I did not honestly think that I was going to be with him in the long run, so I was not bothered. Those were his kids and his problem.

So, I ended up having the test performed and it took a little bit of time for the dye to come out of my fallopian tubes, but eventually, it did and when it did that was a sign that my tubes may have been blocked a little bit, but they were now open. This was great news, which meant that I could become pregnant. So, the next step was getting on some sort of medicine that would allow me to ovulate more, which would cause the eggs to drop.

The Baller seemed to be serious about us getting our relationship back on track and us having this baby. However, I soon discovered he was still up to his old tricks. One night as I got up to go to the restroom, I happened to go through his cellphone and found text messages and naked pictures from some girl calling him 'Daddy' and saying how she missed him.

We got into several arguments over the next several weeks because I discovered it wasn't just this particular female, but others from the past as well that he was still having dealings with while supposedly trying to get our relationship back on track and have a baby.

I decided there was no point in trying to work things out with someone who just wasn't willing to respect you and put in enough effort to show you that this relationship is the one that they want to pursue.

So, although I was not actively looking for a relationship or to get to know anyone, one ended up finding me. I was promoted to Data Entry Supervisor at my job and was no longer working as a canvasser. The Baller would sporadically pick me up from work on an inconsistent basis.

In the summer of 2007, while walking to the bus stop, I would notice a group of guys on motorcycles as I would walk past the gas station to get to the bus stop. One evening after getting off work I was sitting at the bus stop and this guy rode past me on his motorcycle. The next thing I knew he turned around and parked in the parking lot behind the bus stop. I was thinking to myself 'Oh gosh, I really hope he does not come over here and try to talk to me,' but as luck would have it, he did. So, he started out with casual conversation, and I mean he was pretty easy on the eyes, but at the same time, I just really wanted to get home and was hoping that the Baller didn't ride by and see me talking to him in the midst. I ended up finding out that he was the superintendent of a local charter school. Hmm, what a change from the 'thugs', I was used to dealing with but what possessed him to want to talk to me?

Although I really did not want to be bothered, I was curious. I had never explored the side of dating a guy who was not in the streets and who was making a good living legally. I laughed to myself, but over the course of the next few weeks, I could not seem to get this mystery guy out of my head.

So, one day I decided to send him an email. He replied and that evening we ended up talking on the phone for hours. As we are talking, I was in the hallway of my apartment because I needed to listen for the door just in case the Baller showed up. Yes, although he did not pay my bills at my apartment and without him even being in my presence, he still possessed control and fear over me.

Over the next several months, the 'mystery' guy and I would talk on the phone and I would go over to his place after work. I eventually began to have casual sex with him as well. I call it casual because he had a girlfriend, I had a boyfriend, and we still linked up and had sex occasionally. I am not sure from which set of eyes you are reading this book or where you are at this point in your life, so some of you may realize what I am about to say and some of you may not.

At this point in my life, I had moved from being physically abused by others to abusing myself. I was now at a point where I did not realize my own worth and therefore, I allowed others to abuse my body. The body is sacred. We are created in God's image and therefore, should take care of ourselves internally as well as externally. If we are created in Gods image and our bodies are a temple, then that means we reside within God and God is within us. If you think about it in that context, just think about how much we disrespect ourselves with the things that we do. I disrespected myself with sex, some people disrespect themselves with food, others with violence, or self-mutilation, etc. However, what did I know about taking care of my body when I did not feel loved? I didn't love me! I did not know what love was period.

In my adolescent and teen years, I had not seen what a healthy relationship looked like to know how I should conduct myself or how I was supposed to be treated. So, due to the lack of information coming into my environment on how to have a healthy relationship and respect my body I was forced to teach myself by learning from errors which made life a lot more harder than what it needed to be. My reckless behavior of self-destruction was soon getting ready to come to a head because I was getting ready to be faced with some life-altering news. In November of 2007, I was told that I was pregnant.

Lord show me your right way of living and make it easy for me to follow. People are looking for my weaknesses, so show me how you want me to live.
~ Psalms 5:8

Restored: Soul

This was by far the most embarrassing chapter of this book to write. There are so many things that I am not proud to share with you. However, helping you to overcome whatever you are going through by sharing my story with you is worth far more than my embarrassment. However, here is the part that I am happy to write about and that is what I would have done differently. The part where I can leave you with some helpful advice and insight ☺.

So, first things first, There is no cure for daddy less daughter syndrome. If you are a single mother raising a daughter the best advice that I would give to you is to inspire empower, and encourage your daughter.

On YouTube have your daughter listen to one-hour affirmations and then ask her to give you three affirmations about herself for the day. If she is younger than eight, I would say to only let her listen to about 10-15 minutes of the affirmational video since their attention span isn't that long. Then you can give her three affirmations to repeat after you. This is a small exercise in which you can do with your son or daughter to help build their self-esteem and value about themselves.

Put your daughter in groups that are based on girl empowerment, sports, clubs in and out of school, etc. The most powerful piece of information that a girl needs to know is the power of her worth. Girls need to know their value in this world, otherwise, they end up like me sleeping around with men seeking validation and trying to find their value and worth in this world.

If you are not a parent but are in the same situation that I was in I would say to take time out and get to know who you are internally. You are seeking love, attention, and or validation from the wrong outlets.

If you like to write, then write a journal. If working out helps you to think then workout. Whatever your coping mechanism is to help you think I would suggest taking time to indulge in it and think back to who caused you the pain that you are holding onto and embrace that pain. Then let it go so that you can begin to heal from it.

Letting go is not easy. The thoughts do not go away overnight, but what I am saying to you is to start focusing more on what you want for yourself right now. The more energy that you give to your future and your current state the more things will start to align for you in your favor. However, the more you sit and think about the past and the people who hurt you the more energy you are giving to that situation, and the universe will give you more of it.

The universe is big on feelings and emotions because we are a big ball of energy. So, the universe can feel the vibrations of energy that we give off to it. Based on the law of attraction positive or negative thoughts bring positive or negative experiences. So, acknowledge what made you feel that away and then focus more of your time and energy on what you really want for yourself.

I promise that if you begin to look at life from this perspective you will begin to not only heal, but you will bring more of what you want into your life. Often times, people have become so detached from wanting to feel their thoughts and emotions that they drink or utilize some sort of chemical substance. The problem with these coping mechanisms is that you never deal with the thoughts and when you don't have those substances the thoughts are still there in addition to the craving for the drug that you have now introduced to your body.

So, the first recommendation I would make to healing is to find a healthy coping mechanism. You may have one or several. For me, I found coloring, working out, meditating, journaling, and taking a hot bubble bath were all big comforts for me. The next recommendation is to start reconditioning your brain and your thoughts on how you view yourself. This can be done by listening to one-hour affirmation messages in addition to studying the laws of the universe.

The laws of the universe include Law of Divine Oneness, Law of Vibration, Law of Action, Law of Correspondence, Law of Cause & Effect, Law of Compensation, Law of Attraction, Law of Perpetual transmutation of Energy, Law of Gestation, Law of Relativity, Law of Polarity, Law of Rhythm, Law of Belief, and Law of Gender.

There is power in getting to know who you truly are and were created to become. The Laws of the Universe will help you in not only discovering who you are but also to attract things and people who you wish to have in your life.

These laws will help you to manifest your way out of a toxic relationship and into freedom and happiness. Otherwise, you will choose unhealthy behaviors to cope with hard times in life. Also, identify what your coping strategy is currently and determine if it is healthy or unhealthy. If it is an unhealthy behavior, what are you willing to do to change it? Ask God to strengthen you, help you to let go of past hurts and pain, and forgive the person who hurt you. This is key whether you have been in a domestic violence relationship, or you are a daddy less daughter, you must forgive your parent and then ask God for wisdom and insight to move on.

Forgiveness is for you, not the other person. If you do not forgive then you are walking around with past hurts and issues and you create a blessing blockage in your life. Forgiveness is probably the biggest part of healing. You must forgive to begin to heal. Who do you need to forgive in order to heal? What destructive behavior have you overly indulged in because of this person?

Reckless: But Getting Better

So, now that you guys are all caught up on my past, we can now move forward on my journey. Now, would be a good time to pop a bag of popcorn as you buckle in for the next phase of my life.

****

At the beginning of this book, I briefly talked about me finding out that I was pregnant and the Baller being excited. My life appeared to be falling into place. I always wanted to be a mom, but after trying for several years I did not think it would ever happen.

My baby was due July 4, 2008. I had moved out of my little one-bedroom apartment and upgraded to a one-bedroom townhouse with a den in a gated community.

The Baller came to a couple of my doctor's appointments, two I believe. One to determine how far along I was in my pregnancy and then to determine the sex of the baby, which we found out was a girl. He wanted a boy, but I had my heart set on a little girl.

Becoming pregnant still did not stop him from popping in and out of my life. He would stop by drop off some money, spend a little bit of time with me, and then disappear for a week or two at a time. One of the smartest things he did was to give me money and tell me to go open up a savings account and start putting money aside since I would have to go on maternity leave once I had the baby.

I had planned on working until I could not work anymore with my pregnancy. On April 15, 2008, after having intercourse, I felt a feeling of tightening at the bottom of my stomach. I looked up at the clock and I said to myself that these cannot be contractions. I was only seven months pregnant. The pain did not subside and at that point, the contractions were coming about five minutes apart. I woke the Baller up and he touched my stomach and said, "it's just the baby balled up in that area lay down and she'll stretch out". So, I laid down for a moment, but the pain did not go away. So, I got frustrated with him not waking up and I told him I would drive myself to the emergency room. I got up to get dressed and he saw that I was serious, and he finally woke up and got dressed as well.

Once we arrived at the emergency room and the nurse hooked me up to all these machines, poked and prodded, she informed me that I was in active labor. They contacted my doctor and began to administer steroids to help strengthen the baby's lungs and other medicines to help stop me from going into labor. They were not sure if the medicines would work, if not they were preparing to deliver the baby. At this point, they were estimating her to be around 3-4 lbs. The whole time, the nurse is taking my vitals, administering medicine, monitoring the baby, etc. the Baller is in the room asleep. He wakes up hours later asking what was going on and the nurse informed him that I was in active labor and they were trying to stop it. He then says, "I am getting ready to go back to the penitentiary." What????? Why would you say something like that as if I am not already under enough stress thinking that my baby is about to come and is going to be premature with underdeveloped lungs?

Once they got me stable, my doctor informed the nurses that I should be kept overnight for observation. The Baller said that he needed to leave, but that he would come back to check on me. That was a lie. I did not see him until the next day when it was time for me to be discharged. His birthday was coming up and we both knew that he had an upcoming court case in which he was being sentenced and it was possible that they would be keeping him that day. So, I wanted to at least spend his birthday with him. It was weird when I became pregnant, I craved him. When he would leave me, I would cry myself to sleep. I blamed it on my hormones because this was so not me. In hindsight, it also could have been my discernment picking up on the fact that he was getting ready to go to prison for a long time.

After picking me up from the hospital and taking me home, the Baller dropped me off. He did not even get out of the car. I remember going into the house and feeling so worthless. I felt as if he had accomplished his goal of getting me pregnant and now I meant nothing to him. Here I had just gotten out of the hospital.

My doctor had told me that I could no longer work and that I am to be on bed rest and he asks no questions and doesn't even bother to come into the house to get me settled and ease my mind to let me know that everything will be okay. I remember crying because I was so hurt, but more so because I felt so stupid for getting pregnant by him and feeling as if I was just another notch on his belt. Little did I know that day would be the last time that I would see the Baller as a free man for a very long time!

And after you have suffered a little while, the God of all grace, who has called you to his eternal glory in Christ, will himself restore, confirm, strengthen, and establish you.
~1Peter5:10

Restoration in Progress

If I could turn back the hands of time, I would have waited until I was married to bring children into the world. When you are married, one of the sole purposes is to reproduce and create a family. Both you and your husband are striving to take care of the family unit and leave behind a legacy for your children. However, when you have children out of wedlock, it makes the situation a little more challenging. Neither person is bound by marriage, and often the woman ends up raising the child alone. By alone I mean mentally, financially, emotionally, physically, and spiritually.

The Baller was a good dad, but he seemed to believe that being a great dad consisted of just providing financially. So, he hustled in the streets to do just that and he saw quality time as a hindrance to keeping his pockets lined with cash. I am not saying that you should marry the person in which you have children, but what I am saying is that you should take some time and investigate the person who you are dating before you have children with them. How do they treat their mother? This is often a sign of how he will treat you. How does he treat the women in his life (sister, daughter, female cousins, mother of his children, etc.)? If he has other children, how does he treat them? Does he spend time with them? Once you observe and get to know the person in which you are dating take what you have learned about them at face value. Believe what they have shown you. Do not make excuses or try to continuously give them a pass for their behaviors. If you take what is shown at face value, it can save you a lot of heartache and pain in the long run.

Had I listened to what the Baller had shown me, I would have left him before we had even gotten started in a relationship. There were signs of aggression early on that witnessed between him and other people. I noticed that he did not like to talk about his family or growing up very much. Paying attention to the small details of a person can tell you a whole lot about their character. I love my daughter, but I feel if I would have taken the advice that I am giving to you right now I could have given her not only a father, but a present father to raise her, love her, and give her that time and attention that only a dad can give to his baby girl.

Reckless: Welcome

My doctor placed me on a mandatory bed rest, which meant I was no longer allowed to work and the only thing I was allowed to do was to go to the bathroom, take a quick shower and get back into the bed outside of regular doctor's appointments.

Days had gone by without me hearing from the Baller. I called his cellphone repeatedly cursing him out. My cervix was thinning out and it was imperative that I stayed off my feet. Every time I stood up the doctor said it was placing pressure on my cervix causing it to thin out. I was a little over seven months pregnant, but not quite eight months and it was too early for her to come out. My sister and my aunt had fallen out and my aunt asked if my sister could come and stay with me for a while. For some reason, I have a hard time telling people no at times and so, I told her that was fine.

I was very hormonal when I was pregnant. So, I cried over everything. I would hear my sister on the phone saying different things about living with me, so I tried not to be in her presence, and for the most part, I would stay in my room or asleep on the couch. I was stressed over this situation and the fact that I had not heard from the Baller.

One day, I got a phone call from him. It came from a local county jail. He informed me that the day he went to court they sentenced him to four years and kept him. He would be leaving there soon to be sent to the state prison where he would serve out his time. I was so upset. My unborn daughter would not see her father when she came into the world, he wouldn't be home to see her take her first steps, he wouldn't be there to establish that bond that babies need in their early years of life. THIS WASN'T FAIR! I had wanted a baby and I wanted to be a mom, but not like this... How could God give me something that I had been wanting, but not give me the whole and complete package?

I did not get to grow up with a mother and a father. My mom died when I was six and my dad as you read earlier on, left soon after. I did not grow up having the Cosby household, but I wanted it. I felt so confused.

I wondered if perhaps this was my way out of the relationship with the Baller. Maybe this was God's way of telling me that I wasn't meant to be with him and that it was time to move on with my life, but if that was the case why not allow the Baller to get locked up and me to remain childless? Did I manifest being a single mom into my reality?

Your words have power and the universe is always listening and waiting. Our thoughts are energy and wherever we focus our time and energy we can manifest those things into our reality. I had thoughts, dreams, and conversations about having a daughter. I was determined to have a baby and at one point I said that I would have one at any point necessary and I did not care who I got pregnant by.

If I would have been taught that my words do have meaning and that I was the director of my own movie called life, I would have manifested a different reality. For years, I questioned God and why he would allow such a circumstance to happen to me, but I now realize it was not God who had allowed that situation. I put myself into that situation due to my own lack of knowledge of the power that I possess. The human experience is all about learning, opportunities, and failures. The universe doesn't control us at all, but instead, it allows us to choose the things that we want or think best suit us at the current time in our life.

****

My aunt had a cookout at her house for Mother's Day 2008 and she invited me over. Even though I was supposed to be at home on bed rest, I went anyway.

Early in the morning the next day around 3 am, I woke up and felt something wet. The first thing I thought was I am 23 years old 'I know, I didn't pee in the bed'. I can laugh about that now, but it was not funny at the time. I got up and there was fluid coming out of me, but it did not feel like it was coming from my bladder. I went to the bathroom and I was trying to make myself pee, but nothing came out. However, when I stood up the fluid was still coming down my legs.

This is when I realized my water must have broken. I called my aunt and I explained to her what was happening, and she agreed that my water must have broken. She told me that she was on her way over to come and get me to take me to the hospital. I called my doctor and informed him, and he instructed me to go to the hospital and to have them call him when I arrived, and he would be on his way.

Upon getting to the hospital and getting checked out, they determined that there was a tear in my amniotic sac. My doctor arrived the next day and told me the bad news, which was that I would have to now be placed on a level 4 bed rest, which meant I would be kept in the hospital until I delivered.

We decided that we would try and keep the baby in as long as we could and deliver her at 34 weeks. So, for the next two weeks, I was confined to a hospital bed and only allowed up to take a shower and use the bathroom.

I tell you this was the loneliest time ever. I had a couple of my cousins come to visit as well as my aunts, uncles, and friends. However, not having the person there with you, who helped you to conceive, was hard for me to comprehend. No woman wishes to conceive a child just to raise the child alone as a single parent. I sure as heck did not intend on bringing a child into the world to raise them on my own.

I watched the Baller with his other kids and him interacting with them and now my child would not get the chance to experience those sorts of interactions with her father. See that is the thing about living a 'Street Fairytale'. The Baller had money and was able to buy whatever he wanted, when he wanted it, he was cashing out women left and right including the mothers of his children. He was able to do it without punching a clock and he basically, was the CEO of his own business. He ran everything, he risked his freedom for it, and he reaped big earnings. However, with the 'Street Fairytale', there is an ending. An unplanned retirement, that does not happen on your own accord. Thankfully, his ending was prison rather than in a casket.

Despite him being in prison, he was still able to make a couple of moves, due to there being money still owed to him on the streets. He called up one of his friends and had him bring some money to me in the hospital. It was around $3000. This was money to be used to finish getting things for our baby, as well as to continue paying rent and bills while I was off work. So, despite other factors that stressed me out during my pregnancy, money was not one of them. My doctor came by the hospital every day to check on me and to update me as to my progress.

The day had finally approached, and they were planning to induce me on Memorial Day 2008. The evening before I was to be induced, I got a phone call from my cousin asking me if I had seen the news. I told her that I had not seen it. She informed me that the Baller was on the news, him, and some girl. The Feds had gone and raided an apartment that they had together and seized drugs and money. I was upset because I did not know he had an apartment with another woman. It turns out it was the same woman who I had previous arguments with over the phone about the Baller. I can recall her telling me so vividly 'if he is your man then go ask him who I am'. Now, here she was plastered all over the local news stations and facing drug charges.

I was confused by what I was hearing because I thought that the case that he was locked up for was all he was currently in trouble for and then I found out that there was more!

I called up one of my friends who was coming in the morning to be with me and asked if she could stop and grab a newspaper. When she arrived the next day, I found the article, which stated that the Feds had seized vehicles, drugs, and money amounting to almost three hundred thousand dollars in street value. They were also stating that if convicted he could be facing up to 30-40 years and that was on several different charges.

I cried because it was a possibility that this child would never know her father. What have I done??? That is all that I could ask myself. Was it worth it? Why couldn't I have fell in love with some nerdy, school guy? How did I end up here? I wanted the street thug and that is what I got; however, now my wants were causing someone else to start a life off that was not fair to her.

I was getting ready to bring my daughter into the world without her father around. She would not get the chance to know what it felt like to run into her daddy's arms when he walked into her classroom to pick her up from daycare. She would not have her dad there to cheer her on at school performances. I grew up with my mom briefly and without my dad consistently. Now, that same generational curse that was on my life was getting ready to also be on my unborn child, as I prepared to raise her alone. My only prayer was that God did not take me away from her like he took my mom away from me!

After 15 ½ hours in labor, I welcomed my baby girl into the world on May 25, 2008. She weighed in at 5lbs 3.8oz and she was 17½ inches long. After all the hell I had been through leading up to this point, she came out and she was perfect. She had all her fingers and toes, no deformities, and was breathing on her own. We kangarooed for a while before they took her to the neonatal unit to be assessed for additional care. For those who do not know what Kangarooing is, it is a bonding technique where the mom and baby lay skin to skin. The baby's chest is pressed against mom's. Studies have shown it increases the bond between the mother and the child and helps to strengthen premature babies. The baby has been hearing mom's heartbeat for nine months, well 8½ in my case, so the skin to skin contact allows the baby to still hear mom's heartbeat immediately after coming out of the womb.

I loved every bit of it. I loved her smell and just looking at her. It was like unwrapping a gift on Christmas and you find that it was the toy that you always wanted. I never wanted to put her down.

Due to her coming six weeks early, they took her down to the neonatal unit where she stayed for two weeks. She had a brief period where she suffered from jaundice, but after putting her in a little incubator with some sort of artificial lighting she was cured of it.

I learned that when babies are in the womb, they learn the technique of how to suck. Have you ever seen an ultrasound and the baby is either sucking on their thumb or their fist? Having a baby showed me just how perfectly designed God created each one of us. In the womb we learn how to suck, so that when we come out we can automatically latch onto the mother's breast or the nipple of a bottle for some babies and begin to receive the nourishment that our bodies need to grow and sustain itself.

Well, my baby girl did not stay in the womb long enough to learn this technique, so they had to teach her how to suck. Until she learned the concept, she was being fed through a feeding tube. However, even at birth she showed the world just how stubborn, and strong she would be. Apparently, she did not like the feeding tube down her throat and would snatch it out of her nose. I promise you I am not making this up. This less than a week-old baby would grab ahold of the feeding tube and snatch it out… lol. The nurse told me, "yes, she does it all the time. She doesn't like it".

After two weeks of going back and forth to the hospital to visit my baby, pumping milk around the clock for her to drink, I had finally gotten the phone call that she was ready to come home.

Upon getting her home, I remember looking at her and saying, "welcome home baby. It's just me and you".

After I had the baby, I soon discovered that the $3000 that the Baller had dropped off for me was gone! I suspected that it was one of my cousins who had come to visit me while in the hospital. She had asked if she could borrow some money to get her hair done and I told her "no" because it was not my money. Ironically, soon after that the money disappeared. This meant that I would have to cut my maternity leave short because I only paid the rent up for three months with the other money the Baller had given me to put into the savings. I was so upset. She denied taking the money and of course, the Baller had some choice words to say to her.

Having your first child, you expect that this would be the happiest time in your life but for me, it was the worst year ever. My child's father was in prison serving a state bid and facing charges on a federal case and my cousin that I trusted stole a nice lump sum of money from me. I cried every day for months.

Luckily, I qualified for a program called WIC. That allowed me to get my baby formula for free. After returning to work full time, I was no longer eligible for Food stamps, so that was another hurdle. I was making $11.50 and trying to take care of myself and my daughter. I did not live in government housing and have yet to this day apply for it. So, making $11.50/hr. and trying to take care of a newborn on my own; as you could imagine, made things tight financially.

One good thing was that before the Baller went to prison, he purchased me a car, which he paid for in cash. So, I did not have to worry about a car note. Yes, this is the third car he purchased for me. My first car was a Dodge Neon and let us just say I wasn't the most experienced driver and I ended up wrecking it. The second car was a Nissan Altima. I never had anyone tell me about keeping up with the maintenance on a car. I had been driving the car around without an oil change, and the motor ended up locking up causing it to need a whole new engine. So, between the period of having the Altima and the Honda Accord that the Baller purchased for me, there was quite a bit of time that had passed. He likes to say I was on car punishment.

After my daughter had reached six weeks old and had her first set of shots, I decided to take a trip to go and visit the Baller so that he could meet our daughter. He was incarcerated in a state prison that was about 45 minutes to an hour away from where I lived.

I remember sitting in the visiting room, looking around at the walls, the gates, the ceiling, and thinking, is this really my life? Is this what I am getting ready to endure for the next several years? Is this really going to be my daughter's norm for her father? I found this to be so sad and, on the inside, I was crying as I tried to stay strong externally. I looked around at all the other families smiling and enjoying the time they had together before the guards yelled out "visitation is now over".

I looked up at the Baller as he held our daughter on his chest as if he never wanted to let her go. Looking at him, I could tell he was thinking the same thing. He later told me that he could not believe that he was back in prison. He knew like I knew that our daughter was getting ready to live the first years of her life visiting her father in prison. Although, he stated he did not want her to see him like that I informed him that if she did not visit him, she would never know him. I did not want him to come home and she did not know who her dad was and crying because she thought he was a stranger. Even though he was in prison, I wanted them to have a bond, so that when he did come home, she would be excited to spend time with her dad outside of the four prison walls. Excited to go to the park, show her dad off to her friends, and do normal things that kids her age do with their dads. I wanted her to have the chance to experience what it felt like to have a dad. I wanted to give her a gift that I never got the chance to experience.

At six weeks old she was already experiencing things I had never experienced. She had both of her parents by her side and vowing to always be by her side despite our own differences. See, the Baller may not have been the best boyfriend… true, however, he loved all his children and they mean the world to him.

The Baller thought that if he was providing for his children then he was doing great as a parent. Yes, as a parent you are supposed to be a provider. However, there is more to parenting than just providing. You must nurture children; they need to know that you care and that they are loved. They need to feel those emotions from both their mother and father. Love does not have a monetary value. So, that may

56

mean taking an hour of your day to go and see your son play little league football, or an hour to go have a tea party with your daughter. These are memories that will last your child for a lifetime.

These are things that I had to express to the Baller about his other children. He had children by nine different women and so that is many personalities to have to juggle and some women were easier to deal with than others. Some accepted the fact that the relationship had ended and that they were just co-parenting, while others still thought that there was some glimmer of hope of him being back in a relationship with them. So, due to the different personalities, the Baller picked and chose which kids he would be around more than others due to the mere convenience of less stress on him in dealing with their mothers.

However, as I explained to him, you do not get to choose which children you're around more than others. You gave up that right when you laid down and had unprotected sex. Well, he would have plenty of time to think about what I was saying to him as prison became his reality over the next four years.

The Feds had been watching the Baller and were building a case on him. They were at his sentencing for his state case and soon after him being sentenced they filed charges on him for his Federal case. So, in September of 2008, the Baller was bought from the state prison to the county jail where he would begin to fight the charges that were filed against him in Federal court.

The only good part about him being in the county jail versus the state prison was that it was much closer. In the state prison, he was able to hold our daughter and our visits were for four hours. However, in the county, you waited in a long line out of the door to get processed in for a visit. Once on the floor, there were four or five windows that were made from a really thick, dirty, blurry glass. There would be other people having conversations too, which made it hard for you to hear.

He sat in the county for a year before he was sentenced. He watched our daughter grow up from behind the glass. Her learning to sit up on her own, he watched her as she was learning how to walk, and watched her as she tried to reach for him wanting to touch him, but couldn't due to him being behind a glass. We found out that he had been sentenced to 9 years Federal time and the time was to run consecutively with his state time. This meant that after serving his four years in the state prison, he would then be transferred over into the hands of the Marshalls to begin serving out his Federal time. So, altogether he was looking at 13 years!! He tried explaining to me that with good time, a drug program, time served, and a couple of other things, it would come out to him only having to serve four years Federal time. Well, although that was a little better and my daughter would be eight and still an adolescent rather than a teenager, it was still as if someone punched me in the gut. This was not what I signed up for when I asked to be a parent. God, you have the power to do all things. Make this go away!

I prayed it was a mistake, or that something erroneous happened in the case and it was thrown out and he would be released. Although the Baller and I had a couple of bad times in our relationship, I still loved and cared for him and we had far more good days than we did bad.

Back when this was taking place I felt as if he was a source of protection for me. Even if he were not at my house every day, if anything went wrong, he was just a phone call away and would be there to handle the situation. Now, my source of protection was gone. I felt so alone and scared at the same time. Not to mention, I had never been a parent before and now I would have to do that on my own as well.

Shortly, after being sentenced he was sent back to the state prison and our new life was getting ready to begin. I remember people asking me if I planned on waiting for him or if I planned on putting my life on hold for him. I did not know what I was doing. I did not know what God had planned for my life. Well, back then I did not know that I had a choice to choose and create my own reality.

I could have chosen to move on with my life and for my daughter to meet her father when he was released, but I know how it felt to grow up without a father and I did not want her to feel that pain.

Despite, all that the Baller had taken me through I also thought about him as well. How would I feel to be in a lonely prison cell with aggressive men and no one on the outside checking on me? So, I ended up making the commitment to take my daughter to visit her father and for them to stay in touch and I also committed to staying by the Ballers side and helping him financially and emotionally to get through his time.

At that point in my life, I was waking up and living but had no direction or purpose. The $11.50 I was making on my job was not going to be enough to take care of me and this little girl. I decided to go back to school and finish my Bachelor's degree. I enrolled at Franklin University and worked by day and attended school by night. Thankfully, for Franklin, they offered a blend of online and campus-based courses. So, I would take one course on campus that I felt I needed more help in and then take my remaining courses for the semester online. This worked because I would only need a babysitter at night once a week. My aunt was a really big help to me. She had raised my sister and me after my mom passed away and now here, she was also helping me to raise my daughter.

After changing my degree around several times, I decided on a degree in Business Forensics. It would allow me to investigate white-collar crime. I always knew I wanted to do something involving criminal justice, but I was not exactly sure how and to what depths I wanted to be involved, so this was perfect. I could investigate fraud, take it to the employer, and then it would be in the employers' hand as to what they wished to do with the evidence, and should they decide to press charges, I could be called as an expert witness in the case to discuss my findings. I never thought that I would be attending a business college getting a degree in an accounting-related field. I just knew I needed to choose a career that would support my daughter and I and accounting was a safe, reliable, and income-driven career path.

What I did not know was how the universe was using this degree, the situation with the Baller, and my experience as a whole to shape a much bigger picture for me that would ultimately end up helping so many others in the end.

So, what should we say about this? If God is for us, no one can stand against us. And God is with us.
~Romans 8:31

Restored: Welcome

One of the biggest lessons that I learned since that chapter of my life was that I hold so much control over what occurs in my life. In those moments, I thought that God had placed me in those situations. However, I realize that in this world we all operate off the universe's cause and effect law.

I made a conscious decision to become pregnant at any cost and by anyone. The Baller made a conscious decision to make fast money illegally. The result from our choices was that I would now be a single mother raising a child without her father and the Baller would be in prison for a bit of time and miss out on the growing up of his daughter.

Be honest with yourself right now and look at your life. What decision have you made that has caused you to be where you are today? It is not easy to be honest with ourselves. In our society, it is much easier to blame someone else for our misfortune or blame it on the 'devil'. Our words have power and our mind is the most powerful tool on the planet. If you can control your mind and sync it up with your heart you can manifest your version of the 'best' life.

One of the first steps in living our best life is to identify the enemy within. What negative thoughts are you telling yourself? What have you believed about yourself? Who told you those things? Let us take some time right now to work on getting rid of those negative thoughts. Take a piece of paper and make two columns. Label one column Negative and the other Positive. Now I want you to write down every negative thought that you have told yourself or that someone has said about you in the negative column. In the positive column, I want you to write down an affirmation that goes against that thought. So, if in my negative column I write I am fat. In my positive column, I would write I am the best weight I have ever been. I maybe 300lbs, but telling myself that I am at my best weight, I can picture myself at my best weight and it makes me more motivated to strive to achieve what it is that I believe about myself and how I see myself. If I continue to tell myself that I am fat, then I will continue habits and traits that affirm what it is that I am believing and telling myself. It is the self-fulling prophecy.

At the end of the day, God does not want us to be single mothers raising children alone and being a mother and a father to our children. This was not how the family structure was designed. A man is supposed to be the headship of the family unit and be directly connected to God to be able to lead and provide for his family. The woman should be able to trust her husband enough to allow him to lead the family, while she takes care of and nurtures the children into adulthood.

Our society has gotten away from that design of a family and hence, the number of single parents has increased substantially. It is imperative as women that we find our inner voice and discover our power that lies within.

In order to hear your heart speak, it requires you getting moments of quiet time alone, meditate, exercise, color, paint, or whatever you need to do to quiet your mind. Once you are at a place of serenity begin to write and write whatever comes to mind. Do not judge what you are saying, do not try to perfect your writing. Just allow the thoughts to flow. Continue to do this for some time, and then go back and read over what you've written to pick up on patterns. You will notice that your heart is trying to reveal something to you. You want to make sure that your heart and mind are in sync to hear God and to act on what it is that he is leading you to do. However, you should never be in a situation where you are allowing the circumstances of life to just happen to you and you are accepting them. If you notice that things are not going the way you would like for them to go, that is the time to pay attention and see how you can do things differently. Whenever you have those feelings of discomfort it is typically because we are trying to do something in life that does not align with what God has set for us.

So, looking back over this chapter and period in my life, I wish I would have sat down and wrote out a plan for my life. That plan would have included how I would get those things I desired. I should have spoken them to myself every day and believed in my heart that I would have them. This process would have changed my life for the better and caused me to avoid a lot of heartache and pain. The Bible says, 'write a plan and make it plain'. We cannot go through life blind and allowing life to lead the way. God said, 'my people perish for lack of knowledge'.

We must have a vision and a plan for our lives. Otherwise, we will continue to run into the same situations, relationships, etc. What plans do you have for yourself? What is the vision that you have for yourself? It is okay if you don't have all of the answers right now, but at least start writing down something and as you gain more knowledge and experience you can continue to tweak the plan or change the vision!

Reckless: Spiritual Awakening

Besides enrolling in school, I had also found a church to attend. When my daughter was five months old, I had what they called a "Baby Dedication" for her. It is remarkably like a Christening. There were words spoken over her and me. Another milestone of her yet so young life that her father was not present for and it would be one of many to come.

What I didn't realize is that although my life seemed to be a chaotic mess from me in the hospital, my money being stolen, and a host of other situations of confusion and madness, it would be this very chaos that would bring me into my purpose in life. It would be these very situations that would help me to build character and endurance I like to think of it as a pumpkin. When you buy a pumpkin for carving; it is dirty, may have blemishes on it, but you do not care because none of that will matter once you have carved out a masterpiece. So, you wash off the dirt, and then you cut a hole in the top so that you begin to pull out the pumpkin seeds and the rest of the stringy insides. Once, you have the inside all spanking clean, you begin to carve. Depending on your skill level you may sit for hours carving something cool, or you may do something simple.

At this point in the book, God is helping me to heal from the inside so that I can stand before the world confidently and give it the gift which I was sent onto earth to provide. However, I do not believe that we are ever a finished masterpiece until the day we take our last breath on earth. Then and only then does God stop carving out the greatness in you because at that point you are a finished masterpiece and your work on earth is complete. When you're chosen by God, you're dirty and you have blemishes, the universe leads you to water to begin the process of erasing everything you thought you knew so that you can come up new and truly understand the link between who you are in the spirit, your job in the physical (human experience) and how the two need to pay attention to the universe to guide you and lead you to where you need to be. Some people may refer to this as being 'conscious or woke'.

If you are familiar with the seven Chakras some may call it the awakening of your third eye. However, you look at it, it is a process in which your mind is being transformed and you no longer think with old ideologies. This process is when you begin to take on a new mindset.

There are very few people in the world who get to this point in their lives. Most people are living life blind or in a fog. They are easily led by the media, social trends, and are not seeking knowledge. Many of them attend church because that is what they were socially conditioned to do, but they aren't really seeking the knowledge to understand the teachings or understand the true wisdom of who God is and who God is within them. However, in order to hear God and what has been planned for your life and truly experience abundance, it will require taking on a new belief system and stretching your mind past a state of comfort.

When you are ready God will lead you to the right people, places, reading material, videos, churches, etc. You will know when God begins the work in you because you will not think the same, your walk is not the same, your talk is not the same. Things that once made you feel good no longer make you feel the same. Things that once got a reaction out of you no longer get a reaction out of you. Now, this is not an overnight process, it may take years to transform you. The timing is based on our own obedience to listen and adhere to what it is that God is trying to do in your life.

I am one of the hardheaded types that must bump her head to learn that it hurts. God will try and tell me that it is going to hurt, but I am like, well it might not if I do it this anyway. I am sure I make God laugh a lot.

Well, in my former days because I always thought I knew everything. That is probably where my daughter gets that attitude from today. However, I wish they would have taught me in church that because I am made in God's image that makes me a divine god entity as well. I think that had I known and truly let that thought sink into my consciousness, I would have treated myself differently.

In September of 2010, I was laid off from my job. I was told that my position was eliminated, after working for this company for four years! Talk about devastated, lost, and confused!

Now, what was I supposed to do? I had just paid to move into a bigger townhouse because me and my now two-year-old daughter had outgrown our one bedroom with a den townhome and needed more room. So, we were moving to the sister property next door, which was a two-bedroom and was also a gated community.

Well, I have never been one to lay down in self-defeat. I do not like looking at myself as the victim. I prefer to be looked at as the victor! I got up and went to the library every single day to use their computers to send out my resume. The Bible says, 'faith without works is dead". Meaning, you are supposed to have faith that God will provide a way and most importantly believe that it will be done. You should be able to close your eyes and visualize what you need and believe that you will receive it.

If your lights are about to get shut off, you cannot just say "Well, I have faith that God will provide a way". How can a way be provided if you are not moving? So, that may mean calling to see if you can get an extension, asking to borrow the money, going to your local community action agency to try and get help, etc. In all these things you are moving and at that point God can maneuver around to open some doors and make a way to ensure your lights do not get shut off. God can and will make a way, but we must be moving while having faith. That is exactly what I was doing when I got laid off from my job. I applied for unemployment and food stamps to help us stay afloat. I was at the library for 5-6 hours every day sending out my resume and applying for jobs.

The universe has a way of working things to your benefit. I spoke into the atmosphere that $11.50 was not going to be enough to take care of me and a baby, so I enrolled in college. Getting laid off was a blessing in disguise because it allowed me to apply for other jobs that paid more money than what I was making previously and hence without even knowing it, my words were working for me on my behalf.

Many times, if we are comfortable in a situation then we will not move, and had I not of gotten laid off, I would probably have continued working at that company until after I graduated from college. As I stated earlier, I do not like going outside of my comfort zone, but God was putting some things in place that were going to stretch me beyond my level of comfort.

Well, going to the library every day ended up paying off. I had a job within three weeks of being laid off. It was a temporary assignment through a temp agency working in a data entry position for a global logistics company. I had been working there for four months and the company liked me and wanted to hire me on. However I ended up getting hired at a local community action agency working as an Emergency Assistance Representative. The job entailed me assisting low-income families with utility assistance. I loved that job. It was extremely rewarding. I got to talk to various people. I helped those who would come into my office in tears thinking their utilities were getting ready to be shut off or had been shut off. It would bring me such joy when I was able to tell them that we paid to have their services restored or that we stopped their disconnection and placed their bill on an income-based payment plan that they could afford. People would be in tears and want to hug me. They were so grateful. It made my job worthwhile to know that I was able to help another human being that was in distress and I loved that feeling. I have always enjoyed the feeling of helping others.

I remember being in the store one day and there was a man and lady who appeared to be on drugs. The man appeared to be out of it and the lady was in there trying to help him pick out some personal hygiene products. I do not know what drew them to me, but I was drawn. As I was paying for my things, I purchased a gift card that could be used at the store. I found them in the store and gave them the gift card. They were so grateful. The man shook my hand and said, 'God Bless You, Honey'.

I used to think that God disguised angels to test our hearts at times. I now know that it is simply the Law of Compensation at work, which is sowing and reaping. It states that you will always be compensated for your efforts and your contribution whatever, it is, however much or little.

I always try and listen to that voice on the inside of me when it comes to giving and helping someone else. I believe that we all have that voice on the inside of us, however, some listen while others choose to ignore it.

In the Bible, Jesus is referring to the day of judgment and how the righteous will inherit the kingdom. He says *"For I was hungry and you gave me food, I was thirsty and you gave me a drink, I was a stranger and you welcomed me, I was naked and you clothed me, I was sick and you visited me, I was in prison and you came to me"* Matthew 25:35-36. The people asked Jesus when they did such a thing and his response was *"Truly, I say to you, as you did it to one of the least of these my brothers, you did it to me"* Matthew 25:40. God is energy and he lives among us all. He is within each of us. So, when you clothe the naked, visit the sick, visit those in prison, you are visiting God because we are all spiritual entities in which God spirit resides. So, that is why we have urges to help someone else or you feel something on the inside of you nudging you to help someone else. It is the God on the inside of you who recognizes the need of another person and is using you to meet that need. I think it really brings joy to God when he sees humanity working together and helping each other the way he designed them too. I believe that each of us was created for the purpose of someone else. So, if we are withholding our gifts from the world, then we are essentially withholding someone else's blessing. How many times has someone provided you with an unexpected blessing?

If your answer is never then it is quite possible that someone else is not acting on what God put into them to do and thus are holding up a blessing from you. It could also mean that you are not yet able to receive the blessing that the other person has in store for you because you have not yet given your gift to someone else who is in need of it.

I can give you one example, if you are reading this book, I am sharing intimate pieces of my life with you to help encourage you on your journey through life. If I chose to be lazy or disobedient to God in writing this book, I could potentially be withholding information from you that will help to release you into another phase of your life.

****

In the midst, of working at my new job and helping people, I was still in school pursuing my business degree. In 2009 or 2010, God started to drop into my spirit to start a nonprofit to help families who were raising children with an incarcerated parent. I knew nothing about a nonprofit. At the time, I was not even quite sure why he would say such a thing to me. I was not business savvy. I was used to going to work for other people who had established companies and now he was asking me to start a business all on my own to help other families and to build an agency from the ground up.

I was all for the helping other families part of the vision, but running a company on my own, uh, no. God, you must have my assignment mixed up with someone else, someone who was way smarter than me. At least that is what I thought at that moment.

67

I now realize that energy grows where energy goes. So, if I tell myself that I am not smart enough, then I begin to believe that I am not smart enough. However, the idea stuck with me, so I would get online and do a little research as to what a nonprofit was and how it worked because I was confused as to how a nonprofit made money if it wasn't for a profit. God then allowed me to find a place in which I could volunteer and learn more in-depth knowledge of what it took to run a nonprofit.

So, I volunteered at a place that was helping men who had recently been released from prison. They mentored these men and helped them to readjust their thinking from prison back into mainstream society, as well as helped them to create resumes, do job searches, and obtain work. This was in the hopes of getting them back onto their feet and keeping them out of prison.

I volunteered with them for a couple of years and then I tried to step out on my own. Let us just say that was an Epic Fail... lol. Everything that God does he does in perfect timing, which falls under the universal Law of Gestation.

The Law of Gestation states that there is a period of incubation that all seeds need to grow before they can be harvested. Our thoughts, desires, and goals must mature over a period of time before they are manifested into our reality.

I tried to avoid this law and I quickly realized in life the things that are worth having do not have any shortcuts that come with them. I realized years later God was not finished with providing me with lessons to help me to become an effective, strong, and successful leader within a company.

The universe knew that I was capable of creating and running a company, but in order for me to gain the confidence to believe that I could, I had to go through a series of trials and tribulations that would force me to dig deep within and pull/rely on my inner being. During those times, I learned and was constantly being downloaded with knowledge.

While working at the community action agency, I got a chance to talk to many people, and in casual conversation, I would mention starting a nonprofit for families who are raising children with an incarcerated parent and they all loved it and said how they could use something of such service. Working there also gave me more insight into how to run a nonprofit and some things not to do as well.

After graduating from college in 2011, I was actively looking for a job in accounting to get my feet wet and to gain some experience underneath my belt.

To reward myself for graduating from college, I bought myself a brand new 2012 Honda Accord with only three miles on it. It was a definite upgrade from my 1995 Honda Accord that we had been getting around in for the last couple of years. Heck, this car had keyless entry, heated seats, an auxiliary plug, and more. This was the first car I had purchased for myself and I was dang proud.

In July of 2012, I began getting the urge to just walk away from my job. I was nervous due to not having a job lined up before leaving. I mean I had increased my income by .50. I went from $11.50/hr. at the basement finishing company to now making $12/hr. at the community action agency. Was I really supposed to walk away? Then something inside of me just told me to walk away and not to look back and that is what I did. Thinking back on it, I can relate to Abraham when God told him to leave his home country but did not give him the full details of where he was to go. At the time, I didn't know that this urging feeling that I kept feeling to leave my job was God and that this would be my first and certainly not my last time of hearing the voice that would be leading me to what was in store for me.

I left on a Friday and did not return that Monday. I ended up leaving the community action agency in 2012 and began my journey into the field of accounting. I did not land a job right away. So, I ended up taking a temporary job working at a warehouse making $9.50/hr. I was stressed out. I was afraid I mistook my own voice for God's voice. What had I done? I have a child to care for, rent, bills, and not to mention a car note.

I was so relieved when I found a job about a month later that was in a suburb about 30 minutes away from my house, working as an Accounts Receivables Specialist (Fancy word for Collections). I got the job through a temp agency making $13/hr. That was $1 more than what I was making at the community action agency. After 90 days they liked me, and they wanted to hire me on permanently with the company. They offered to pay me $16.83/hr. I was ecstatic!! That was the most money I had made yet in my career.

I worked there until July of 2014. I began to grow bored and not to mention stressed. I was literally a bill collector. I had to find out the reason invoices were not paid and then I got reprimanded if I did not collect the money in a certain timeframe. I did not like being responsible for someone else not paying their debt. Plus, I did not go to school to do collections. Not only was I growing bored with the work, the distance was becoming an issue as well.

At least once or twice a week there would be an accident on the freeway causing traffic to slow down. Traffic in that area at 5 pm could be awful. Many times, I would have to call cousins or my aunt to go and pick up my daughter from afterschool care. You know how that can go. Eventually, people get tired of you asking and they stop answering their phones when they see you calling at 5 pm... lol. I do not blame them because I can be the same way when I am tired of doing something. So, I began trying to look for something closer to home. The job was becoming more stressful.

My accounts were looking great, and my boss thought that they looked too great and so she began to pile more difficult accounts on me, which dropped down my collection rate. She would then make threats to me saying things like 'if you don't get those accounts collected, I would hate to see you go, but you know we have fired other people in the past for the same reasons'. I have never been fired and I sure as heck was not about to give her the satisfaction of doing so.

I left that Friday and on Monday, I gave her my 2-week resignation letter. Just like the last time, I left and did not have anything lined up. Now that I was on my spiritual journey with God, I realized that all great leaders started somewhere. Many times, God does not propel you without a struggle. I guess you can say it is the Law of Polarity. You must see both sides of a situation. Yes. I left a job without a job and I had bills to pay; however, by leaving it, I was now opening myself up to receive a job that would pay more and allow me to be closer to home. This would allow me to avoid being stuck in traffic and not having to rely on people to pick up my daughter from childcare.

We must take time to value and appreciate every step along our journey in life because they are all interconnected and have meaning to get you to where you need to go. I appreciate the time that I worked as an Accounts Receivable Specialist because it gave me additional experience in the accounting field, and it opened the door for me to get into the field. The pay also set the bar to allow me to begin to negotiate my salary rather than taking what was offered.

Sometimes we can be so blinded by what is in front of us that we miss the picture as to why we are in that situation. Every situation in our life has a given time, purpose and season. We must learn to listen to God in order to navigate through the various situations in our lives. That sounds good as I am writing; however, it would take several more years before I began to live out what I just wrote.

****

So, after leaving the Accounts Receivable position, I ended up landing a couple of temporary jobs that were much closer in distance to my home, until I got a better opportunity.

In October of 2014, I began working for a Japanese Manufacturing company that just so happened to be less than ten minutes from my house, which was so amazing!

During this time of my life I was not familiar with the Laws of the Universe but looking back on it now I can see that I attracted this job to me. My vibrations were high in that I was dissatisfied with my last job due to it being so far away and being hard to get my daughter from childcare, so the universe bought me a job that was closer and paid more to make up for me having to leave a job that too far away, but paid well. This new company had a small office, which was good because I would have the opportunity to do more and learn lots.

At this point, God had been working with me and teaching me how to read his word in addition to going to church. Going to church is nice and you leave feeling whole. However, by Monday or at least the middle of the week, you're feeling discouraged, and your spirit feels under attack. My pastor says that we need God's word to have a constant covering and something to throw back at the devil when he tries to attack us mentally, spiritually, or physically.

The 'Devil or should I say the enemy (Inner Me) is constantly attacking us and telling us what we cannot do, who is better than us, lie after lie after lie.

I am sure you are familiar with the voice of your enemy, that voice that says what you cannot do or who is better than you or that you're inadequate, etc. It is important to know and learn the word of God and how to interpret it, so that you can apply it to your daily life and become a better version of yourself and discover your purpose here within the earth.

The more I began to read the Bible, the more I felt myself establishing an intimate relationship with God. Through reading the Bible I began to pray more and talk to God more. I found myself having an open dialogue between God and myself after reading some of the things from the Bible. I also found myself being more accountable for my actions.

I am sure that you are aware that you are a two-part deity. You are human and you possess your spirit. However, we can get so convoluted with what is going in our outer world that we neglect to feed our spirit and it is the spirit that holds many of the answers in which we are searching for in our outer world. My pastor likes to say we have our flesh man and our spirit man. The Bible teaches us that we should feed our spirit man and allow the flesh man to die, which allows us to establish a much deeper and richer connection to God. You are killing off the way of the world and taking on the mindset of God and strengthening your godly divinity that resides within you. You may be doing this by reading your Bible, meditating, researching theological knowledge, etc. Our bodies are temples in which God resides and so if God resides within our temple (our body) then we should take care of it.

Take a minute and think of your relationship with God and what it means to you. Now, think about how you treat your body. What do you feed it, what do you drink, what do you allow people to do to you? Would God approve of those things? If you answered no, do you realize who you are to God and who the universe is within you?

The more I read my Bible the more in tune with GOD I became, so much so that I am now able to hear that small still voice when it speaks to me and know that it is leading me and guiding me. Correction, that voice has always been speaking to me I just did not realize that it was God/my inner being speaking to me.

Each and every one of us has an inner being that speaks to us no matter where we are in our spiritual journey in life. For instance, have you ever been out with a group of friends or met a person and you get a really bad vibe about that person? You do not know what it is, but you're picking up bad vibes from that person? Next thing you know you hear about that person killing someone or raping a woman, etc.

I have had that feeling more than once around certain people I have met, but that feeling is God talking to you and protecting you. It was God who was urging me to leave my job when I worked at the community action agency. Had I not left, I would have still been stuck making $12/hr. It was him who revealed to me in 2007 that I would become pregnant by the end of the year. Not only did God speak these things to me, but I agreed with what I heard and was intentional about manifesting them int my reality.

There is a thing called "Purpose" and "Destiny". In July of 2015, God told me tha it was time! Time for what you are probably thinking. It was time to start the process of bringing the nonprofit into a reality. God had revealed to me that there were women in prison who cried themselves to sleep because they missed their children. Children were hurting because they missed their parents. There were men whose parental relationships were being broken down due to them being absent and that the time for this nonprofit was now!

As the Universe revealed this information to me it was as if I could feel the pain o the women in prison, the pain of the children who had an incarcerated parent, as well as the pain of the fathers. Families were waiting for me. Kind of like the Israelites wh were slaves in Egypt. Their freedom depended on Moses being obedient to God's wil and leading them into the promised land. The story of Moses and the Israelites applie to all of us. We are all Moses. We are all here on earth and assigned to free a different group of Israelites. I discovered that I am assigned to free youths, at-risk youths, and youths who have been impacted by having an incarcerated parent. I could no longer allow fear to delay me from my assignment.

Often when God gives us an assignment, the universe is not looking for the most qualified. We were all designed specifically for our assignment, so we are already qualified. The universe created us with the ability to get the job done and will provide us with all the necessary resources to accomplish our tasks as well as reward us along the way.

When Moses was leading the Israelites to the promised land, during their travel they defeated tribes of people who were far larger in number and size. The same is true for us as we are on our mission to complete our assignment. Your assignment is to help the people in which you were created to help and ultimately when they receiv that help and their need is met and the change is evident by the fruits in which they are now bearing you essentially have gotten them to the promised land.

However, before you get them there you will be met by many obstacles that seem insurmountable. There will be things that stand in your way that seem bigger than you and fear will set in and tell you that you are not equipped to go up against those challenges, but like Moses with God by your side and God residing within you, anything is possible. If he gave you the assignment and the task it is simply up to you to believe that you can and are able to do it. If you have the slightest bit of doubt you will not accomplish the task. You must believe it and feel it. You must feel like you have already succeeded even if you have not started the task yet. You are the creator of your own reality and when your energy and vibrations are in alignment with the universe there is nothing that is impossible for you to achieve or possess.

This is the pep talk that I gave to myself as I took the first step and I contacted a company called Legal Zoom to file all the proper paperwork to get the nonprofit established.

In July 2015, Unlocking Futures was established. I was so excited, but I had no idea the hard work that was in store for me in terms of getting an organization off of the ground and taking it from an idea that was in my head to an actual organization owned and operated by me.

Remember the amazing things he has done. Remember his miracles and his fair decisions
~1 Chronicles 16:12

Restored: Spiritual Awakening

This chapter was the beginning of my transformation and at the end of 2019, I heard God tell me that in 2020 it would be my year of transformation and isolation.

I am not a numerologist, but from reading the Bible and picking up on patterns in my own life I can tell that God and numbers have a special relationship. It appears that every 10 years in my life God is transforming me. It has now been 10 years since was given the idea of launching a nonprofit that is now known as Unlocking Futures. When I started writing this book three years ago, I had left the Japanese Manufacturing company and now here I am getting ready to share this book with the world and I have left another job that I have been at for three years to begin working at Unlocking Futures full-time. That has been a dream of mine since I incorporated it as a business.

So, knowing that transformation happens daily, but specifically every decade I am trying to be more cognitively aware of what and how I utilize my time on the earth. I have found that the key to being blessed in life is by being a blessing to others. It is the universe's Law of Compensation that I spoke about earlier.

I have paid people's electric bills when I had a disconnection for my own, gave at church when it was my last, fed the homeless in the dead of summer, etc. However, what I have found is that it is in those times that you are depositing into your 'in need reserve. There will come a point in your life when you need something. It does not always have to be financially, but it could be health-wise, or needing favor in a new business venture or career.

The universe has a way of turning around and rewarding you for the time that you were selfless and gave unto someone else who was in need.

Regarding my spiritual journey, it is still a work in progress. However, this year I feel as if I have been placed into a spiritual cocoon. I have shed old beliefs and thinking and taken on a new spiritual perspective on life. I feel as if I am learning how to navigate this human experience with more clarity. I am learning that I truly am in charge of my reality and that I can create it however I would like it to be and all I hav to do is sit and quiet my mind and focus my intentions on what I want. If I give it enough focus and energy it comes to me.

When I meditate, I listen and I move on what I am supposed to do when I come out of my meditation. One of the biggest discoveries on this spiritual journey has been to realize that God is not a deity in the clouds sitting on a throne watching me, but he is energy always surrounding me and lives within me and he wants me to live an exuberant life and lifestyle. I no longer look at the devil as this big scary creature that is red with horns, but I look at the enemy as the inner me who is in constant battle with the person in which I can be and who I strive to be. So, reading the bible, praying, and meditating are all things that help me to decrease the lies and thoughts of the inner me, so that I become who I was created to be.

Becoming the person, you were created to be requires transforming your mind. The Bible references that when you chose to follow Christ you let the old you die, and you put on a new version of yourself. Simply put, whenever you're going after a higher version of yourself, you will need to let old ways and thought patterns die and be willing to embrace new thoughts, patterns, habits, etc., that will get you to where you are trying to go. Trying to get to a higher version of yourself cannot happen if your embracing old thoughts and ways. The definition of insanity is doing the same thing and expecting a different result.

Earlier, I spoke about our 'Inner Me' which we identify as an outside source that some call 'the enemy' or the 'devil'; however, it's a battle within ourselves and can be found in the prefrontal cortex of the brain and the limbic system or lower part of the brain.

The limbic system served our ancestors well when they had to hunt, endure extreme weather, etc. They lived in the flight, fight, or freeze mode consistently. However, as we have evolved as humans, we have found that to live in this state all of time is unhealthy for us mentally, physically, and emotionally. Despite our evolving, the limbic system part of our brain does not want us to evolve and would prefer we stuck to what we knew and that is how many times we find ourselves living or reliving past situations that no longer serve us in our present state.

What situation/s are you reliving, what situations still bring about fear when you think about them? Now that you are aware of them, what can you do to keep moving forward? What goals do you have set for yourself to achieve? Each time, a thought from the past comes up just remember that its your limbic portion of your brain trying to keep you connected to the past and keep pressing forward to create new pleasant memories. Eventually, you will transform what your limbic system knows as the past because you will have re-written your story!

The Reckless Baller

Things were beginning to fall into place for me. I was growing into my own woman, molding my mini-me into being a strong little woman, and God was still working on showing me who I was and whose I was daily.

I am sure you guys are wondering at this point, what happened with the Baller? When I last spoke about him, he was serving out his state prison term after being sentenced to nine years of federal time. His time was to be served concurrently, meaning after he did his state bid he would be taken off to do his federal time.

During his state term, I would take my daughter down to visit him every other weekend. This became our new 'normal' over the course of the next four years. In fact, it became so normal that my daughter at the age of two would yell 'My daddy's house' whenever we passed by abandoned warehouses.

Although there is no easy way to normalize prison, it became the only thing my daughter knew to be the home of her father. Luckily for us, he was placed in a state facility that was family-oriented. By that I mean, they had a park with swings, a slide, and a mountain climber. In addition, to the park they had picnic tables, so during the spring and summer, we could take our food from the vending machine outside and have a picnic.

The Baller would take my daughter and put her on the swing as she screamed for her mommy when he would push her too high. Then after he took her off the swing, she would make him repeatedly go down the slide with her as that was her favorite piece of playground equipment.

The Baller and I grew a lot through these visits. I guess you could say we grew a lot through our pain over the years. Although I would take our daughter to see him, I had a lot of unanswered questions; I had a lot of unresolved pain in which he caused that I was still harboring inside of me. His friends eventually dwindled down to one by the end of the first or second year of his sentence. They stopped answering their phones, no one came to visit, and no one sent him any money. His world became him, our daughter, and me.

It even became a challenge to stay in contact with his other children as their mothers felt this was a mistake that he made and they weren't going to take time out of their lives to take their children to go and visit, nor were they willing to take money out of their pockets to put on their phone for him to call. Did they have a right to feel this away? Absolutely. Was it what was best for their child? Absolutely not! Children were not created by the mother solely and therefore, despite the father's mistakes that child still needs their other parent. Fifty percent of their DNA comes from that other parent. So, although we may hold some resentment towards the parent for whatever reason, we as adults have to put those feelings aside and do what is best for our children. Otherwise, children of incarcerated parents tend to draw on the conclusion that they were left and abandoned by the other parent. They may then build up resentment towards their parent causing the relationship to deteriorate and make it hard to be repaired upon the parents release from prison. This will be the Baller's reality when he is released. Some of his children wait in anticipation for him to be released, while others it will take some massaging of the relationship before it is fully repaired if ever.

Now, let me add that if the parent is incarcerated for committing a violent offense towards the child or the child's caretaker, or any other violent act in the community that would make it unsafe to have a relationship with the parent I totally understand and the verbiage about maintaining contact doesn't apply to you. This is for parents who feel as if they are no longer with the person so, they do not make any efforts for their child to maintain a relationship with their other parent.

However, being a daddy less daughter, the best advice I gave to the Baller regarding his other children is to allow them to heal at their own pace. You cannot force the healing process and you must validate their pain! It is due to his choices in life that he ended up incarcerated for an extended period causing him to miss out on important times in their lives. So, as the parent, he will also have to be patient and allow them to heal and a part of healing is venting. In doing so, he will hear things about himself that he is not pleased to hear however, these are the opinions and feelings of his children and he must validate them for the healing to begin.

****

After the Baller's realization that the person that he had been unfaithful to, treated unkindly, and even abused at one point; was the only person still in his corner, he began to have a life awakening moment. Like I said, he always loved and cared about me, but when you are on the street, and you have the money, the cars, the jewelry, women come along with that as well. He was able to get any woman that he deemed fit.

I remember telling him one day that if he did not have the money, the bling, the cars, and was just an ordinary person walking down the street, those same women would not look twice at him. He laughed and said, "so, what you trying to say? I'm ugly because I am not no ugly dude". No, that is not what I was trying to say. The Baller thought that he was on top of the world. He had many of the things that hard-working middle-class families strive to obtain and a selection to choose from any woman of his choosing.

In a Biblical sense, he would be compared to a wealthy royal, Pharaoh, etc. Many of these men were wealthy and with wealth came a hefty appetite to have many concubines in addition to their wives. Concubines often wanted to be with these men for their status as well as for the opportunity of having him provide for her financially. Thousands of years later, this mentality has not changed and holds true in this era as well.

Many of the women who were attracted to the Baller or had slept with the Baller were only attracted to him for his status and to have him take care of them financially. Love was not a factor! I do not judge these women as they were simply products of their environments. Men like the Baller were essentially equivalent to them working a job. They used their beauty and body to obtain money to take care of themselves and their children (if applicable). For many of them they may not have had successful businesswomen to look up to, so how do you become something in which you are not accustomed to seeing as a norm?

Over the course of the next four years, God began to take the Baller through a Joseph encounter. He had found himself in prison, alone, and broke. He had been stripped clean of anything that would allow his lips to form the word 'I'.

A couple of years into the Baller's prison term, he began to realize what he had been given in me. I was more than just the mother of his child, I was more than someone he once lusted after and then fell in love with, he realized that I loved and cared about him. He realized that in me he had a friend, someone in which he could confide in. The moment he realized what he had in me was a life-changing experience for him. The love that he was receiving from God through me was something the Baller was not used to having in his life.

I realized that his failed relationships with women were due to the relationship that he had with his mother. I will use our relationship as an example, when the Baller began to fall in love with me, he expected me to feel that same deep-rooted love that he felt for me. However, we were moving on two different scales. He was more open to allowing himself to love me, where I was more reluctant to open myself up to him or anyone else right off the bat. I did not grow up with parents, so my level of trust and being able to show affectionate feelings while in a relationship lacked the same level in which my partners gave to me.

The Baller on the other hand grew up with both his mother and his father. However, after his father left the home, some situations occurred between his mother and him that shaped his view towards women in an unhealthy aspect. I believe that subconsciously he treated all women as if they were his mother, hence the reason his relationships were unsuccessful.

The Baller found it easy to fall in love with me, while I found it a hard-vulnerable emotion to show and to give, but when I do finally open up to someone, I love hard! The more vulnerable the Baller began to become with me, the stronger our bond became. He began to divulge truthful answers to all questions that I may have had regarding his dealings with other females. By doing this it broke down my insecurities and I began to become more secure in our relationship. I can't explain the feeling to you of having someone blatantly lie to your face and you know they are lying because you can feel it deep down in your gut and then have the person look you in your eyes years later and tell you that you were right or for them to explain the situation to you. It's an exhilarating feeling.

Slowly, I began to fall in love with him again. It was as if we began to get to know each other all over again but this time I got to know the real Baller. He was looking at serving a 13-year prison sentence, so we had nothing but time to take it slow and get to know each other as we began to grow through our broken pieces. We were two broken people who had become broken along the way in life due to totally different reasons.

So, upon our meeting, we knew that there was a deep mutual attraction, but due to meeting each other in unhealthy mindsets, we endured situations that could have been preventable. We were both wounded from past situations and came into a relationship with swords and daggers out and slinging the words 'I Love You' around as if they were going out of style.

However, through the Baller's incarceration, our broken pieces became whole and like a puzzle, we began to put our whole pieces together. The Baller vowed to never lie to me again and to be upfront with me. He said that he would never want another woman to think that she held information about him that I did not know and that she could use this information to hurt me. So, he said that no matter how painful the truth may be he vowed to always tell me. That is exactly what he did.

As we had the hard conversations about his dealings with other females, although I knew it to be true, it still hurt like heck. He would gently wipe my tears away and say, "I know it's hard to hear it and I hate that I hurt you, but I don't want to lie to you". That for me earned him a second chance.

The person that he was morphing into was someone that I wanted to get to know more. It was a person that I wanted to be more intimate with as I shared things with him about my past, present, and future thoughts on life. I had never had this type of honesty with any man that I had dated.

Many people have said or may think that the Baller is only saying these things to me because he is incarcerated and to these people, I would say "you must have never dated someone who has been incarcerated". I am not saying that there are not some women and men who are incarcerated that are not cons and they prey on people's feelings to have companionship and or to get money to take care of themselves. However, this is not the case for the Baller and me, who were together for five years before his incarceration. We had history. A very rocky history, as you have been able to see. So, to see him change right before my eyes, when he did not have too was absolutely nothing but God's hands working on his life.

You cannot make anyone change, no matter where they are in life. A person will only change when they are ready to change. God has a way of getting our attention when we choose not to be obedient to his will. We cannot outrun God's calling on our life.

While the Baller was incarcerated, he began to develop a spiritual faith in God, and he began to have dreams for his life and for us as a family. When we dream it is said that we are seeing things from the spirit realm. If you can think of it and see it, you can manifest it into your reality. However, if you do not deal with or let go of what you are hearing from the enemy (Inner Me) you will be manipulated into believing a false reality. The voice of the enemy is often so loud that it keeps you from knowing what God is taking you through. Sometimes, while on the course to achieving God's purpose we are given some tests/trials that we must go through. These tests/traits are not meant to hurt us, but to build our character and strengthen us for what is coming up next on our life's obstacle course.

I believe that God chose to sit the Baller down and humble him and work on breaking the pride and arrogance out of him. So, every source of money that the Baller thought that he had and could turn to, God shut the door on it, including the $3000 my cousin stole from me at the hospital.

There were times during the Baller's incarceration that he was unable to purchase his necessities on commissary. There were many nights when he went to bed hungry because he did not have the money on his books to buy additional food and snacks on commissary. I tried to help him when I could, but I was struggling myself on the outside to stay afloat and take care of our daughter. However, it was all by God's design that the Baller had nowhere to turn to because it forced him to turn to God and him alone. God was trying to show the Baller that he was not self-sufficient, but that he was enough with God. God wanted the Baller to seek him and to turn inwardly. God wanted to spend time with the Baller and for the Baller to get to know him on a more intimate level.

God had to teach the Baller to hear his voice. So, he took away all forms of comfort and placed the Baller in an uncomfortable situation, an isolated situation, in which he could have the Baller at his most vulnerable point. He put him in a place where he and God could have some one on one time. Had God not set the Baller down and stripped away all forms of comfort to him then the Baller may have never found a spiritual relationship. In fact, he would have been doing his prison time without blinking an eye. He would not have learned from it and sadly, he probably would have a high likelihood of returning to prison at some point in the future.

For God to do the things that he had in store for the Baller, God had to sit him down and work on his mind. I believe that God chose to split the two of us apart so that he could work on the both of us internally. I like to say that he gave us both a Joseph experience with the exception, that I was not physically incarcerated. However, when you're supporting a loved one who is incarcerated it is as if the family is incarcerated too. I will get to that a little later in the book. I felt as if God broke me down to the bottom and so did the Baller; so that he could transform us through a renewed mind.

In the Bible, there are some people whom God used their life as an example to the world to make a point. Similarly, I feel as if the Baller and I had been placed on a pedestal in front of the world and we have had our lives on display. As you read earlier, the Baller's dealings in the street were publicized on the T.V. and in the local newspaper. I was pregnant with my first child but too embarrassed to tell co-workers and people outside of family where my child's father was which led many people to come to their own conclusions.

Going back a little further, recall the big incident that occurred between the Baller and I, when he put his hands on me? I had family, friends, neighbors, classmates, teachers, etc., in which I had to tell my story too. I would have said nothing, but it is hard to explain why your eye is almost the size of a lemon.

Fast forward to my daughter becoming grade school age and making up stories to her friends as to why her dad never comes and picks her up from school. She would tell friends that her dad was a truck driver and he was not home that much. So, not only has the Baller and my lives been on display but so has our daughter.

What I have come to learn is that God must display the ugly parts for the world to see, so that they have something to compare when he puts his hands into the mix and transforms Ashes for Beauty. During this time of transition, he took away friends, family, associates, etc. Both of us had many moments when we felt angry, abandoned, and alone. However, we now know that it was all a part of God's plan. Those people did not leave us, God put them at a distance. They could not get to us in this season of our lives. Upon God completing his work in us, he then put us back on display for the world, but this time we were not be broken, we were be healed in every form and fashion of our lives. Our hearts were healed, our minds healed, our children be blessed, our finances in the best shape ever. God is bringing us out into an overflow of abundance! The world will know the work that was performed by God and him alone.

****

Well, even though the two of us were growing as individuals, I still had some self-healing that needed to be done. I did not realize that many of the things I went through as a child were affecting my ability to have healthy relationships as an adult. I also did not realize that I could not take the things that the Baller had done to me and sweep them underneath a rug and act like they never happened. It would not be until dealt with those pains and hurts that I would truly begin to grow as a woman.

However, before coming to this realization, I felt that I had a right to be vindicated for what the Baller had done to me, and now that he was incarcerated this was my time to make him feel all of the pain that he had put me through.

If you recall earlier on in the story, I had met the 'Mystery Motorcycle' man. Well, he too was still in the picture. After finding out how long the Baller would be away, we ended up rekindling our relationship. It was the Baller who decided to commit his illegal crimes, not me. So, why should I have to become a nun and vow to be faithful and committed to him? This was my rational way of thinking early in the Baller's prison term and I was also in my early twenties.

The depths of the relationship between the Mystery Motorcycle man, and I became a little deeper because we were spending more time together and my feelings grew stronger for him. I believe his feelings for me grew stronger as well; however, he did not want to be in a committed relationship, nor did he want to have any more children outside of the son he already had at the time. Yet, despite knowing this I continued with having a sexual relationship with him.

It was not okay for me to accept the fact that a man only wanted to be with me sexually but had no desire to commit to me. My body is a temple in which God resides and I was disrespecting my dignity and body each time I had sex with him. Even though I knew this to be true, I did not feel it in my heart. My mind knew this to be true, but my heart and mind were not on the same accord, which explains why I lived in confusion for so many years over this situation.

At the time, I still was not at a point where I fully loved myself, which is why it was so easy for me to give myself a way to others. I did not realize that I was a precious priceless jewel because I did not see myself as such.

Outside, of the Mystery Motorcycle man being a Superintendent for a local charter school, he also was a well-known musician. The more I got to know the Mystery Motorcycle man I learned that he could have an ego at times. He would compare apples to oranges with me about our faith as if because he had been a devout Christian longer than me that made me less than in the Kingdom of God.

However, what I could not understand is how he could have sex with me as well as other women, keep it a secret from his church family and pastor, and yet always seemingly tell me how he has been a Christian longer than me and how I don't want to debate the Bible with him? It is people like him that cause so many lost souls to turn away from the Church and not want to become a Christian. They make you feel as if you are beneath them. They seem to believe that they are higher ranked than you are in the body of Christ.

Over the years, of having sex with the Mystery Motorcycle man, I did not know that there was something called a soul tie. All I knew is that I could not break off the relationship with him. I would say that I was going to leave him alone and then I would find myself right back in the same position and then repenting to God for forgiveness afterward. The more I grew closer to God, I would ask him to remove the Mystery Motorcycle man from out of my life, to make me forget that he ever existed and yet it seemed as if that prayer went unanswered. I now realize that I had the power the whole time to break off the sexual relationship between the Mystery Motorcycle man and me. I was making a conscious decision to give in to lust and ignore my mind and heart which both were telling me that this relationship was not going to lead to a marriage or children.

Sex was created to be a beautiful and intimate moment that brings two individuals together and intertwines their souls making them one. Hence, when a couple gets married the officiator of the wedding announces that the two people will now be joined to become one. However, if you are not married, sex still works the same way; the only difference is that you begin to intertwine your soul with unfamiliar spirits. You then begin to do things that you did not used to do, and you may find it hard to break off the emotional connection with the person. This friend is what you call a sou tie!

Earlier on in the relationship between the Mystery Motorcycle man and me, I would pour out my soul to him via letters I wrote, text messages, emails, etc. and each time he would gently try to break it down to me giving me a different reason each tim as to why he didn't want to be committed.

I can recall the last time I expressed my love for him, and he was not so nice. He explained to me that he was trying to finish up his doctoral program and that he had other dreams and goals that he would like to accomplish and settling down in a committed relationship, was just not something he wanted to do. He informed me that the last long-term relationship he was in, he ended it because the lady could not understand or value the fact that he did not want to be in a committed relationship.

The closer I became to God; he began to reveal things to me via various outlets. I remember the first time; I informed the Baller of the relationship between the 'Mystery Motorcycle' man and me. I had told him that I no longer wanted to be with him. I told him that I found someone smarter and more educated than him and I wanted to be with him. After telling the Baller about my hidden relationship, he told me that if that is what I chose then to go right ahead. He said that I was being used for sex and was not getting anything out of it. He said, "At least if you're going to sleep with him you should be getting something out of it. Have that dude pay a bill or something". His comments struck deep and made me feel cheap. I felt used. The visits after he found out that piece of news were a little awkward. He would express to me how he felt about me and that I was the only woman that he wanted to be with for the rest of his life. He said that he could have other women if he wanted to. In fact, a couple of them had been writing him and he had spoken to a couple of them on the phone but told them that he was in a relationship with me.

We were expressing so much with each other during this time. Even though it had been a couple of years since the Baller and I had been sexually active, there was still a deep-rooted emotional connection to him. However, now I had also intertwined a second soul within me in addition to the Baller. For several years, I prayed to God to help me in my confusion. I was so confused. I now know that the confusion was due to my heart and mind not being in sync. I did not know if I was supposed to leave the Baller to be with the Mystery Motorcycle man, was I supposed to leave the Mystery Motorcycle Man to be with the Baller, or was I supposed to leave the both of them alone to make room for someone greater than what either of them had to offer me?

The fact that I had so much confusion about which of the relationships to choose as well as feeling guilty, should have been a clear indicator to walk away from both relationships, but I continued to struggle with making the right decision for me as well as for my child. I now know that when you are in alignment with the universe and what it has for you, you will not feel confused, but at ease. So, that is why it is so important to pay attention to your feelings and use them as a guide to lead you to what it is the universe has in store for you.

As a rule of thumb, remember that if it comes from God it does not come with chaos and confusion, but with peace, joy, and love. I should have decided to leave both relationships alone and start fresh with who God had specifically for me.

As hard as I am on myself about the situation, I also am learning that it occurred this way for a reason. I was 18 going on 19 when I first met the Baller. I had little relationship experience. The Baller was only the third serious relationship that I had ever been in. I was very inexperienced in the love department; however, by being involved with the Mystery Motorcycle man it allowed me to see the difference in the love that I received from the Baller and what I was receiving from the Mystery Motorcycle man. The love from the two of them was different, but both of them provided me with some valuable life lessons. Lessons that I could take with me as I continued through life and onto finding a healthy loving relationship one day.

****

Although I started to see small changes in the Baller, anytime we would get into an argument, if he called me out by my name, or raised his voice at me, I was quick to say "See, you haven't changed. You're still the same person that you used to be". I was constantly slinging his past in his face. How could you say that you love me, and you want to be with me and you're the same person who blacked my eye and punched me as if I was a punching bag at the gym? But you love me, right? Finally, he had enough of me bringing his past up, and he said to me "I don't know what else to do to show you that I am a changed man. If you do not believe me, I cannot force you to believe me. I am not the same person that I was when I was home. I have watched you grow and mature as a woman and I know that for me to be in your life, that I too must grow and change. I can't come at you the way I used too; otherwise, it's just going to push you away".

He was right! God began dealing with me and he spoke to me one day and said, "Ashia, how can you continue to bring up someone else's past when I forgave and forgot about yours". Wow!! Can you say, 'hit me like a ton of bricks right in the face?' That moment and then after I stopped bringing up the Baller's past. I was still confused as about whether I was supposed to continue in a relationship with him or if I was supposed to move on. Was I potentially preventing a relationship from occurring with the Mystery Motorcycle man and me? He had told me once that he was afraid to get into a relationship with me and then the Baller comes home, and I end up going back to him. He said that he had that happen to him before and that is why he was afraid to get in too deep with me. I told this to the Baller, and he said that the guy was full of it. He said that if you absolutely love and care about a woman, nobody is going to stop you from having what you deem to be yours. Nobody!

Let us just say I did a lot of praying about this situation between the years of 2008 2015 - the four years the Baller was doing his state term and into the beginning of him starting his federal time.

I enjoyed spending time with the Mystery Motorcycle man, but I was so conflicted with my feelings. I loved both men, but I knew it was not right and that I could not continue to be with both men. I was finally becoming honest with myself and that was half the battle in making a good decision. How could I be upset that the Mystery Motorcycle man did not want to be in a committed relationship? That was his decision just like it was my decision to continue to have sex with him. So, in making the decision of which relationship I should choose and which one to let go I was feeling conflicted, but the answer I was seeking was lying dormant within me.

I think that we often know the answer to some of our most difficult situations, but we do not like the answer or the choice that would need to be made in order to resolve the situation. Therefore we continue hoping that the situation will work out in our favor, however, it doesn't and often the situation can escalate and get worse if we don't leave when we are supposed to.

I truly realized the growth of the Baller on a visit one day when he told me that all he wanted was for me to be happy and that if that meant me not being with him then he was willing to let me go. He told me he appreciated me riding his time out with him this far and that we would always remain great friends even if we did not work out in a relationship.

You would have to know the Baller to realize how exponentially huge of a moment it was to hear such words come out of his mouth. The more honest and genuine he became the more attracted to him I became. It was as if we were getting to know each other all over again. It was as if someone pressed a replay button on our relationship.

Not many people are given the opportunity to start over fresh in a relationship. In our society, so many people want microwave relationships. They want the fairytale wedding and the prince charming without ever having to put in the work. All relationships are going to require work. It is all a matter of when you wish to put in the work. It may come before marriage or after.

Personally, I would much rather go through the tough times before I marry a man rather than during my marriage. I value marriage and hold it in a high and sacred regard and therefore, once I say, 'I do', I plan on staying married. There is no divorce! My grandparents were married for over 50 years and it wasn't the perfect marriage as I believe no marriage is, but my grandmother stuck it out with my grandfather even though he cheated on her and she had biblical grounds for leaving him, but she didn't. She stuck it out until my grandfather took his last breath on this earth. I want that type of love.

So, although the Baller and I went through some very ugly and tumultuous times in our relationship, I am blessed that God cherished me like his own daughter and set the Baller down and basically told him that if he truly loved and wanted to be with his daughter he would have to start with some internal change. He was giving the Baller a second chance, but this would be the only chance that he would have to get it right with me.

90

Yes, God loves us like we are one of his own. We are one of his own. He created us in his image, so he loves us just as he loves himself. He is energy around us as well as within us. Although I was a daddy less daughter, God protected me. I went through some ugly domestic violence relationships, but I did not die, and I do not look like what I have been through.

In fact, there are going to be some of you who know me who may read this book and not even know that I went through domestic violence because I never wore my struggle. I do not believe in being a victim, but a victor. There is power in your words so we must choose wisely how we identify ourselves. So, you will never hear me say that I was a domestic violence victim. I do not identify with the word 'victim'. I prefer victor because in all situations I will always come out on the winning side. I do not think about the 'what if' or the 'should of' or 'could of' in life. I just decree and declare what I want for my life and believe that what I want will be manifested into my reality.

If you can get your heart and mind synced up and working together, you have the power to do anything that your mind can comprehend. If I had knowledge and insight into this type of thinking and believing I believe that I could have prevented many of the situations that I encountered in my life.

Every situation has a cause and an effect. Just as all humans were sent here to help assist each other to navigate through life. If you went through a traumatic situation or any situation for that matter and you made it through and you are in your right state of mind today, you owe it to the next woman to reach back and grab her by the hand and help her out.

Helping someone else out doesn't mean you have to write a book, but whatever your gift is that you possess inside of you that is the gift that you are to use to help those whom you are supposed to reach in your lifetime. I hope that by sharing my experience of domestic violence in this book it gives some woman reading this book the courage to know that you too can get out of your situation and move on to greatness.

After leaving a domestic violence situation, it is important to get counseling for yourself because chances are you endured a lot of trauma during that relationship whether the abuse was physical, mental, or financial. Outside of counseling, you will need to continue to work on you and have moments of mindfulness to reflect on you your past, your future, and your present and decide what you want for your life and how you will make it a reality for yourself.

I promise after a year of counseling and working on yourself you will see and notice a change. You will grow stronger, wiser, and most importantly you will start to fall in love with you. Often, we end up in domestic violence relationships because we, for some reason, lost sight of loving ourselves or we never discovered who we were as a child growing up and becoming a woman.

Once you get to a point where you can boldly declare that you are in love with you, you will never allow another human being to disrespect you ever again because you will be so in love with who you are that on the inside of you, disrespect won't feel right or sit right to entertain a relationship with a man who so much as jokingly disrespects you.

What I will say is this if your significant other stands a chance at changing and you guys working it out, they will first need to seek a relationship with God on their own. Depending on the person, they may also need to seek counseling, and or rehabilitation for drugs and/or alcohol.

Continue to work on getting to know who you are as a woman and allow God to lead and direct your heart. The best way to do this is to be alone. So many times, I have seen women in my life go from one relationship to the next. I used to be like this in my teenage years. It's easier to go from one relationship to the next because then you don't have to deal with the pain of getting over the other person; however, it's toxic because you're not allowing yourself time to heal, so those emotions get buried. The next thing you know the same things that happened in your old relationship begin to happen in your new relationship and it is because we attract what we are. So, it is imperative that before moving onto a new relationship that you work on yourself to take on a new mindset. Otherwise, if you try to move on into a new relationship with the same mindset, then you will encounter the same person just with a different face.

Insanity is doing the same thing and expecting different results. We as women must learn how to be by ourselves and embrace our pain, let go of it, and then start healing from it before jumping into new relationships. Then and only then will we attract what it is that our hearts truly desire. That is probably the best piece of advice that I could give to any woman just from my personal experience in life.

If it is meant for you to be with that person then God will work on them. He will break them down, carve out the bad, and build them up new. We as women are nurturing and beings must realize that we do not have the inapt ability to change the behaviors of another human being. They must first want the change for themselves and be willing to seek the help and do the work to change. Change is possible, but we must first seek to change ourselves, as we do not have the power to change anyone but ourselves.

But Christ died for us while we were still sinners and by this GOD showed how much he loves us.
~ Romans 5:8

Restored: Baller

Looking back at this time in my life with the Baller and the Mystery Motorcycle man made me realize how important it is to take time out for yourself and heal from your brokenness. Being with another person will not heal your most deep and intimate parts.

I also learned about taking time to quiet my mind, so that I could hear my heart speak allowed me to hear God. I do not have the complete blueprint for my life, but I do have a better idea of what it is that I am supposed to be doing on the earth.

I have always enjoyed helping people. That brings me so much satisfaction. I used to wonder why I went through so many tough situations growing up while it appeared my peers were living healthier lives. However, I now realize that every situation that I endured up until this point was meant for me to be able to reach and be relatable to the people I have been assigned to aid and assist on earth.

Everyone who says they care does not care and everyone who says they love you does not love you. What is love? We toss the word around so often and nonchalantly, but do we really know what love entails? Would we know what love is when love appears?

I do not want to give away too much of the upcoming chapters, but what I will say is that the Baller had a way with words and getting what he wanted and needed people to do for him. I call people of such caliber manipulators. The Mystery Motorcycle guy although he had commitment issues, provided me great life advice over the years that I have known him, but most importantly I respect him for never leading me on. From day one, he always made it clear that he didn't see it in his life path to be in a committed relationship and how he had other things in his life that required more of his attention and he felt a committed relationship would deter and or distract him from getting those things accomplished. So, I am disclosing this to you to say, when a man tells or shows you who they are believe them. Do not try to make excuses for them. You will save yourself a lot of heartache and confusion along the way if you would simply listen to what it is that they are telling you. When the right person comes along, there will not be a need to explain your feelings to them because they will constantly be expressing their feelings towards you. They will not hurt you physically or verbally.

So, before you move on to the next chapter, I would like for you to take inventory of all of the people in your life that you have direct relationships with and determine if those relationships are adding value or taking away value from you. Make two columns one labeled 'Value' and the other labeled 'No Value'. Write the names of the people closest to you in the appropriate columns. Afterward, look at the people in each column and then make note of why you have each person in that designated column. Lastly, with prayer and perhaps meditation decide if the people who are not adding value to your life are worth the continuation and exertion of energy. In order to become the highest version of ourselves we must learn to put ourselves first and one way to do that is by taking inventory of our relationships!

A Reckless Spiritual Journey

In May of 2012, the Baller was released from the state prison system and turned over to the U.S. Marshalls to begin serving out the next four years of his federal time. If you have ever been with a man who has done federal time, then this is when you begin to realize that it is not just him serving time, but you and your children as well. He was first sent to West Virginia to begin his time, but this would only be one of many stops on his journey of serving out his time.

Our relationship was still rocky. We were both in the hands of God and being transformed into the parents that we needed to become for this little girl that we were given. On one of the visits to see him, the Baller asked if I had still been talking to and seeing the Mystery Motorcycle man. I replied, 'yes'. He was hurt and upset. He told me that after I left from visiting him not to come back.

Why is it as humans, we can do things that we know are not right, but when someone else calls us on it we are hurt? I knew what I was doing was wrong but hearing him say to me not to come back hurt me. I guess it was me wanting to have my cake and eat it too. I found myself caught in between two men and I loved both. As the Baller told me this, tears started streaming down my face. Our four-year-old was watching me as she pretended to be playing. The Baller took his hands and wiped my tears away. He then expressed to me how he loved me and that ever since he met me, he has always held me to a higher standard than any other woman he has dated. He said there was something about me and he just liked to think of me as being perfect. No blemishes no scars, and especially being someone that no other man had touched, someone that was all his. He explained that is the reason why when it comes to me being involved with any other man he becomes so irate because it's as if someone has knocked me off of the pedestal that he has placed me on in his mind. He did not want, nor did he see me like any other female in the world or should I say his world.

After that visit, I tried to cut off ties with the Mystery Motorcycle man, but it was short-lived. I continued to be sexually involved with him, even though it was not the best situation for me. As I became more spiritually in tune with God there were more and more things revealed to me about the Mystery Motorcycle man that told me that he was not the man for me. I would pour out my heart to him and express how much

I loved and cared about him and how I think that we should be taking our relationship to the next level. His response would always be that he did not want to be in a committed relationship due to the things that he had going on in his life. He had enrolled himself into a Doctorate program and he now made that his focus as to why he did not want to be with me. This was after other excuses before enrolling in his Ph.D. program.

I finally had come to the conclusion in 2015, after him flat out telling me that he didn't want to feel as if I was pressuring him into a relationship, that what I felt for him wasn't what he felt for me. I knew at that point, that this was something that I needed to let go of. I needed to get it into my head that the marriage and additional children I wanted would not be something that I would experience with this man.

I became spiritually conflicted every time I laid down to have sex with him. I was also conflicted because I was visiting the Baller telling him how I wanted to be with him and making plans, but still having sex with the Mystery Motorcycle man.

However, during my confusion what I did notice was that whenever I would go to visit the Baller, it felt right. It felt as if our souls were intertwined into one. I almost felt as if I could feel God smiling down on us when he, our daughter, and I were together.

There were times when there would be something bothering me, and he would just so happen to call me and ask what was going on with me because he could feel that something was bothering me. I was in awe that he picked up on such things. The same would happen for me, I could tell when he was feeling down and missing my daughter and I because I would have these strong urges to see or talk to him out of nowhere. I would then send him an email and tell him to stop missing me so much and he would reply, 'how did you know?' …. lol. When I was around the Baller, I did not have those same feelings of shame that I felt after being with the Mystery Motorcycle man.

After being in West Virginia for almost nine months, the Baller was then transferred to a federal prison in Kentucky. I enjoyed the drive and the scenery of this place, so this was a transfer that I did not mind at all.

My daughter and I would travel to see him but make it a small little vacation as well. We would visit, then go and see a movie, or go shopping. We came to know the town well over the three years that he was down there.

God continued to work on us as individual people. The Baller was now going to church, reading his Bible, and praying as well. Through reading this book, you have come to know his personality and character just a little bit. However, if you knew him in person, him believing in God would be a total shocker to you. This was a man who once told me he believed in a higher power, but he was not sure if it was God. This was a man who was all about himself. I mean arrogant, selfish, and at some point, or another it was if he thought he was a god. It was his way or no way.

In fact, prior to him going to prison, he became my god in a sense. If I needed money, I went to him. I begged for his attention and cried if I did not get it. I was more focused on this man of flesh than I was my Lord and savior. So, it makes complete sense to me now, as to why God had to tear us apart. You had the Baller who thought that he was god and you had me on the other end of the spectrum who thought that the Baller was my god.

Two people who come from and who have endured trauma can only create additional traumatic experiences for each other if they do not take the time to be alone and work on themselves internally. The universe wanted us to have the opportunity at being a healthy and happy family and knew for us to have one then there was healing that needed to take place.

Everything that transpired from 2004 to 2018 had been a part of God's divine intervention. If you recall the incident between the Baller and I that took place in 2004, you could imagine it messed with me a lot. No matter how much, I thought that I had blocked it out of my consciousness, it would arise, and I would think about it. Whenever I would think about it, I would begin to have emotions of hate and disdain for the Baller.

In 2016, I thought I heard God speak to me and reveal what that situation meant for both of our lives. "The future of the Baller and I was going to be so great. The situation that took place in 2004 was meant to kill you Ashia. Had the plans succeeded I would be dead, and the Baller would be in prison for life. Hence, the both of us would die without leaving our imprint upon the earth. One of us physically, and the other mentally". Wow!! I could not believe what was revealed to me. I had dealt with this situation for years. I was embarrassed to talk about it. I was embarrassed for people to find out about it because I was afraid of what they may say or think of me for sticking by the Baller. However, I realized that the destiny in which God had spoken over our lives cannot be stopped by anyone, but us due to our lack of obedience. I would come to find the true meaning of what was revealed to me four years later in 2020.

****

Knowing that even in the midst of a life or death situation, God is still present speaks so much volume about how much God values you and needs you as a vessel on this earth. Every morning I wake up with a heart of gratitude for being alive another day since I know how close we are to death every day. At least I know. You cannot really value and appreciate something until it is nearly taken away from you.

I do not discredit anything that has happened to me. I know that God will be able to use my story to help someone else. Perhaps that is happening right now as you read this book. Our testimony is used to save others. I do not want women who are in domestic violence relationships to read this book and think that it is okay and that if they stay and ride it out things will get better. Otherwise, you could end up in a situation like my mother and have children who are watching, and you do not realize the damaging effects of you staying and how they are affecting your children.

If you are not strong enough to leave, pray, and ask God to give you the strength to get out of the relationship. Think about the long-term effects of you staying and how it will affect your child into adulthood. As a parent, we are the first example for our children, and what we show them will be passed down to their children and will become either a generational curse or blessing.

I was determined to break the cycle of domestic violence in my family. I never want my child to endure a man putting his hands on her or for her to see a man put his hands on me. I know how it feels to be that child who sees their parent being abused.

As you have read, I also know how it feels to be the woman being abused. You are afraid, you are scared, and for me, I internalized all my emotions. I was not strong enough to leave. God intervened as I am sure he will for you, and he stepped in and forcefully took the Baller out of my life by sending him to prison. Both of us were broken and two broken people cannot come together and make each other whole, no matter how hard they try. They will only end up making a whole broken person. This was the case with the Baller and I.

On the road to healing, the first step is for each person to deal with their internal issues and that is what God began to do with me. God loved me so much that not only did he deal with me on what had happened with the incident in 2004, but he also began to deal with me on my daddy issues.

I felt abandoned by my dad and I resented him for it, but at the same time, I kept allowing him in whenever I got back in touch with him. I was only hurting myself in the end because no matter how many times, I let him back in he would be present for a short time and disappear for a longer period. I would get so angry at him that he could be a father to his other children, but not to me. His first-born child! My issues with my dad were showing up in my relationships.

As you can see, I grew up to date men who did the same thing as my father. They would come in and leave as they pleased, and I would accept them back when they came back around. When the Baller was out, he would come around and then disappear for days at a time. The Mystery Motorcycle man would come over one day then disappear for days at a time as well. This was the precedence that I set in my life, but not intentionally. I did not realize that what my father had done to me I was manifesting in my life through my relationships and causing myself unwanted pain. God revealed to me that my dad was only the person that he chose to get me into the earth. He was a vessel. Sometimes, the vessels that God uses are not meant to be a part of the whole plan. Had my dad been a part of the whole plan, then I would not have experienced the pain that I endured, the relationships that I encountered, and hence, became the woman that I have grown to become.

Pain can turn people into some of the most beautiful people that this world has ever seen. They can love like no other human being has ever been loved simply because they know how it feels to be hurt and they do not want anyone else to feel that type of pain. I also came to realize that my dad never learned a healthy mechanism of coping with pain and grief. He liked to drink alcohol and I believe that was part of his coping mechanism. However, he never fully grasped the concept of healthy grieving. The reason I say this is because my mother was the first woman that he ever fell in love with and if you ask either of his ex-wives, they will tell you the same. He talked about her all the time and despite it being 26 years since my mother passed away, my dad still speaks about my mother and where they would be if she were still alive as if it was just yesterday when she passed away.

I believe that whenever he is around me, I remind him so much of my mom that i makes it hard for him to bear and deal with the pain. That is because he has never fully dealt with the pain and the realization that she is gone. Simply because rather than deal with it, he ran from it, and because he ran from it, I missed out on what it was like to have a father.

My daughter is growing up missing out on what it is like to have a grandfather tha she can run to whenever mommy or daddy does not give her what she wants. Pain ha cheated him out of an awesome and amazing relationship with his daughter and granddaughter. However, here I had a God that loved me so much that every aspect of pain in my life he took time out to sit me down when he knew that I could fully understand what he was saying and explain it to me.

Initially, I was hurt and upset about the Baller going to prison, but I now realize that him going to prison allowed me the much needed alone time to focus on becoming a more mature woman for myself, my daughter, and my future spouse one day. God took the time to tell me why certain situations transpired in my life. He ever explained to me that my mom couldn't have stayed in my life longer because she wasn't strong enough to walk away from my stepdad and had she stayed around they would have destroyed God's plans for me!

God chose me to be an example for my family, my child, and women across the world. It would be through my life that God could show these women what freedom looks like after domestic violence. I had been chosen to show the world what a relationship with God looks like when you give yourself quiet time to hear him and you are obedient to follow his directions for your life.

God has placed a gift inside of me that is bigger than me. I am using one of those gifts at this very moment as I am writing this book. It took a lot of courage on my en to sit and write this book and share some of my deepest secrets with the world. I told

God while writing this book, that I did not know if I wanted the world to know some of the things in which I was being urged to place into this book. However, God instructed me to keep writing. On the inside of me, I heard a voice tell me that everything that has happened in my life leading up to this very moment has been predestined. The world needs to know my story so that my story can help someone else to get out.

God brought me out so that I could reach back and show you that you too can get out of your situation. God uses ordinary people to do extraordinary things. However, when you use average everyday people to do extraordinary things it shows people that if it can happen to that person then it can happen to you as well. It provides humanity with hope. Joseph was average, Noah was average, Moses was average, Solomon was wise but like any other human, he had his flaws. However, God used all of them to do some extraordinary things in the Bible.

I now know that God is also using my life to do some extraordinary things. I may not be able to save the world, but if my life helps to save a few lives it was all worth it. I now try to stay in the mind frame that I am not of this world. I am a divine entity here on earth having a human experience. I get my instructions from God through meditation and paying attention to my feelings. There are some things that I do that others cannot seem to understand like quitting a job without having another lined up and not losing anything in the process. If God puts you on an assignment, you can be assured that you will not be sent out into the wilderness ill-equipped or without the necessary things to take care of the task at hand. Meaning he God will supply all your needs so that you can be successful in orchestrating your assignment through to completion.

I think that sometimes as people we have a selfish view of life. We think that we are living solely for ourselves, but we are not. Each of us is living for someone else. Our lives are meant to help other human beings. Even during a bad relationship, your life and experience with that person has helped them in some shape or form. They may not see how during the relationship, but years down the line, they will see how much being a part of your life impacted them. For some people they were solely created as vessels to get others into the world, some were meant to guide the children they bore into the world into adulthood where God would then take over and lead the way, then there are the few who were chosen to change the lives of many. No one was created by accident and no matter how big or small your task is in life; you were created to change the life of someone else. I like to look at it like a row of dominoes. God has lined us all up since the creation of man and he has knocked down the dominoes and as each one falls it affects the other.

I hear many religious people speak about being 'Chosen'. I believe that if you are having a human experience, you were 'Chosen'. However, many people come to earth and they disregard their assignment and they become convoluted with what is occurring in this earthly realm. Then there are the few of us who may have become distracted, but we find our way back to digging deep within ourselves to discover the reason why we were sent to earth and we begin to work on our purpose.

We live in a world where perversion is gleamed upon like a badge of honor and standing up for what is right is frowned upon and looked down on as judging. We live in a society where only the esteemed, educated, and affluent, are worthy of being called a saint, while, the poor, the widowed, the incarcerated, and the broken, are looked down upon. However, these are the lost sheep that God is seeking.

I am on a spiritual high at this point in my life. I am discovering how I am supposed to navigate this human experience and it feels amazing, but now that I am discovering this information, I want to share it with so many women who were like me so that they too can be free to discover their purpose.

I was thinking so hard about how I could go about bringing this information to women and once again that small voice inside of me said that all I needed to be was my true and authentic self. If people can feel and see God's love it is much easier to talk to them about faith. The only way that people will experience God's love is through you. God is in each of us. When someone hurts you, they have essentially done it to God too. If someone blesses you, they have blessed God. Our story is just what God gave us in order to show the lost sheep that we too, were once lost. It makes us relatable to others.

People are more likely to listen and take advice from someone who has been in their situation and came out on top then they are to listen to someone who is still in the situation and struggling like they are to figure it out. We all have a light in us no matter how dark it may seem, you just have to be willing to allow someone to come in and help you carve out the dark spaces, to get to the light. You have a gift inside of you that the world needs at this very moment in time. Your gift is meant to bring someone else out of their situation. Whether you are a gospel singer, rapper, teacher, mechanic, shoe salesmen, etc. We all have a gift. Some are big and some are small, but they are all used for the same purpose and that is to bring people out of their dark situations, and into the light so that they too can receive the inheritance that God has promised to them; Peace, Prosperity, Love, Joy, these are all things that come with being a child of God. Life can be tough at times and it is during those times that we must dig deep within to tap into the God within us.

I promise you that if you make time to quiet your mind and hear from God, your inner being that dwells inside of you, you will find the answers, clarity, and peace in which you are seeking. We have all of the answers to all of our problems, we have the solutions to problems that the world faces, we have the means to be and encompass all that our minds can fathom, but in order to obtain those answers, you must dig deep within. So, while living this life that you were given on purpose and not by chance, ask God to reveal to you what your gift is and where it is to be used. This may not be a quick answer.

It took me almost 30 years before God revealed it to me. I am sure it could have been a shorter process if I knew about meditation, the Laws of the Universe, and that I have the power to create my own reality. The irony in your gift is that it is something you do so naturally. You do not think twice about it. That is how natural it is to you. Allow your inner being to be your tour guide and guide you on this journey called life. There will be some ups and there will be some downs, but it will be a much better life than the one you had before knowing God. That I can promise you!

For GOD is not a GOD of confusion, but of peace.
~1Corinthian 14:33

Restored Spiritual Journey

Wow!! This chapter was seriously a spiritual journey as I learned and grew with God. Since I initially wrote that chapter, God has taken me on another spiritual journey. Much deeper than the first one. This one that I am on now is causing me to dig deep into myself and look at what I was told, how I was raised, looking at these that occurred in my life, and looking at life and death through a different spiritual lens. The more I learn the more it shapes me. There is not much about this chapter that I would change.

However, I would have liked to have had a small group of women who were also on a spiritual journey or a group of older women who had been where I was currently so that we could grow together and get encouragement from each other or so that I could be uplifted by them and given advice.

I believe that had I done these things I would have discovered that God taking the Baller out of my life was for a reason, but because I refused to take my eye off of what I wanted to see rather than seeing what was in front of me it would cause me to pay a pretty high price.

As for the Mystery Motorcycle man, I believe that certain people come into our lives for a season to get us through a part of our lives or to bring us information to help build us up. The Mystery Motorcycle man was a very well-educated business and spiritual man who taught me a lot. However, during the process of teaching me various things, we allowed our flesh to get into the way of things and muddy up the purpose of our paths colliding. I have now learned that it is okay to ask God what purpose a person serves in your life and while waiting on the answer, be patient and don't move or advance too far ahead before receiving that answer.

One of the biggest lessons I have learned thus far in my life is that when you have childhood traumas and then relational traumas on top of that it is imperative to take time out and heal from the inside. You must take time to embrace the pain, let go of it, and begin to heal. Healing for each of us will look differently.

For me, healing means sitting in a tub of hot water, burning incense, and listening to the water fall from my Zen fountain as I listen in silence or sometimes with slow R&B or jazz music playing. Other times, healing for me is coloring as I process my thoughts. Then there are times, I do not feel like talking and I journal my thoughts instead. I have come to learn that the technical term is 'Mindfulness'.

Giving the brain moments of mindfulness has been scientifically proven to heal the brain from trauma as it reduces the size of the amygdala in the brain and helps the body to stop giving off cortisol as the levels of stress decrease in the body.

Once you are in a place where you are feeling more in tune with you and those past hurts no longer trigger a response within your body then perhaps you may be ready to date again. There is not a specific time frame as to when any of us are ready to start dating again after trauma. Sometimes, you may even meet someone while you are in your process of healing who helps you along in your journey. I am not a doctor and nor do I claim to be an expert, I am merely here sharing my personal experience in a hope that it can help someone else. The things that I share are only suggestions as these were things that helped me along my journey when I was dealing with my own chaos also known as life.

Reckless <u>30</u>

Who would have known that through my relationship with the Baller I would end up finding not only myself but my purpose in life? We were together five years before his incarceration and at the point of writing this book he has been incarcerated for 10½ years. He is scheduled to be released in April 2019. This will be the third time that we were expecting him to get out. However, this time sounds more official due to him receiving his report date to the halfway house and some other release procedures being conducted inside on his behalf to prepare him for that release date.

It's been a long road. April 2019 will make 16 years that the Baller and I have known each other. If God would have told me 16 years ago that I would endure the ups and the downs with the Baller and the extent to which I have had to endure, I would have told God I will pass on the experience. Just send me my prince charming. I'll bypass all of the other drama. However, would I really know how to love and respect my prince charming had I not endured pain? Probably not. Had I received my prince charming without the pain I would have probably messed up the relationship thinking the grass was greener somewhere else and cheated on him not knowing that had a good relationship at home. I am just being honest.

I was a broken and wounded little girl in a grown woman's body trying to find my way and figure out life and in the process had my perfect gentleman come into my lif I would have probably caused him some emotional heartache. Hurt people hurt people and as you can see from my story thus far, the Baller and I were both broken; hence, our tumultuous relationship in the beginning.

Then comes along the magical age of 30! Many women say that when they turned 30, they were so depressed because they felt they were officially getting old. However I was excited to turn 30. I had done so much growing internally and it felt amazing. I had come a long way from the things that I had been through. I had been through a lot, but I did not allow any of it to break me. There is something about the age of 30. If you read the Bible, there are several people including Jesus, in whom God ignited their destiny/purpose upon them reaching the age of 30 or older.

As I mentioned earlier, I honestly believe God has a special relationship with numbers. When you turn 30 it is as if your mind is in a place where God can now sta to bestow wisdom, knowledge, and understanding upon you. It is a time when our childish and foolish ways are behind us and we begin to look forward to the planning of our future for ourselves, our children, and our families. We begin to start searching for our purpose in life. Why were we created? What makes us unique? What sets us apart from every other human being on this earth?

If you know God, then you know that he does not use the same mold twice. The more I began to spend time with God the more he began to pour out his infinite wisdom and knowledge upon me. I would find myself praying for wisdom and knowledge like that of King Solomon.

Over the course of almost a decade, I had seen a lot and been through a lot. However, had I not experienced the relationship with the Baller including his incarceration, I would not be the founder of my own nonprofit organization: Unlocking Futures. I would not be in a position of wanting to help other families dealing with incarceration. I would not have an empathetic heart. I honestly believe that Unlocking Futures is my destiny in life. Everything that I have experienced in my life was meant to get me to this point; a point where I could not only help people but feel the depths of their pain.

When I worked at the local community action agency, my former boss told me that one of the things that made me great at my job was that I had empathy and compassion for the clients and that wasn't something that she could teach to the other reps. I believe one can only have true empathy for another person when they themselves have been in the same or similar sort of situation. When you know how it feels to hurt, to be in pain, to be broken, to lose everything, etc., it's at that point where you can truly relate to someone else rather than listen and agree. That is what made me a good rep while working in community action. I did not act as if I was above my clients because I too was receiving help with my utilities. I too knew how it felt to try and do the best that you could but yet it still didn't feel as if it were enough as you worry about how you're going to keep the lights on or trying to decide between paying the light bill or purchasing groceries.

However, the older I get the I am finding that faith is trusting and believing in God even if you cannot see the outcome. It is believing that whatever you want for your life you can have and obtain it. Obtaining it requires that you be able to focus on it and feel as if you already have it. If you can do those things you are able to bring the unseen into your reality and that is where the real God power shows itself.

For so many years, I was taught to pray and wait, but God is waiting for us to realize that we have the power to possess everything in which we desire and ask for. The Bible says we have not because we ask not. If you ask and believe then you already have it. The Bible says that God will supply all our needs and he knows our hearts desires before we even speak.

****

I can recall taking my daughter to visit with the Baller when he was incarcerated in the county jail, and I would hear some of the woman saying things like, 'she has her brand new baby down here in this dirty jail. That could not be me. I wouldn't bring my child down here'. Okay, well that is fine, but this was my life and decision that I chose to make for my family. I chose to put my own needs aside so that my child would know her father. It's women who make those sorts of comments whose children end up suffering. It is those children who go to school and bully other children, cannot focus in classrooms, and are a disruption to the classroom setting, simply because they miss their parent. They do not understand why mom or dad is no longer around or they know where mom or dad are but they are upset that they do not get to see them or talk with them. It is tough for children who do get to go and visit their parent, but when you have a child who has not seen or heard from mom or dad in several years, that can be tough!

Some like to say that you cannot miss what you never had but that is not true, especially, when that person makes up 50% of your DNA. You know that something is missing. A part of you is not physically present with you and you yearn to fill that void. This is true whether the parent was present or absent in the child's life.

Throughout the Baller's time of being incarcerated, I have heard so many stories of women not taking their children to go and visit with their father. However, I have not heard a valid reason as to why. Many of the reasons are very selfish and self-centered and do not focus on the needs of the child. This then causes additional emotional issues for the child who then starts to believe that the parent who is incarcerated has abandoned them and some children develop hatred and anger for the parent while others just yearn to be reconnected.

Meanwhile, the caretaker of the child may notice that their child resents them for keeping them away from their parent. They may show this directly or indirectly. Children who show it indirectly may act out in the community or in school. We as parents must put away our own feelings when we have children and put their needs first.

I recall going and visiting with the Baller when he was incarcerated in a federal prison in Kentucky and we would have to stand outside underneath this tent-like area until they buzzed us into the gate. Once inside the gate, you would have to fill out your paperwork and you still would have to stand outside, until it was your turn to go inside. It did not matter if it was raining, snowing, or 10 below outside, the procedure did not change. That did not stop men, women, and children from going to support their loved ones. Now that is true dedication. That is the true definition of parents setting aside their feelings to ensure that they are raising emotionally sound children by putting their needs first.

However, I would feel bad sometimes, as I would hold my daughter in those cold temperatures, swaying back and forth with her face wrapped in my scarf and my arms around her to keep her warm. Again, those thoughts of 'Why am I in this situation?' would begin to flood my mind. I used to say things like 'this is God's plan for my life. Who am I to question it?'

However, now I realize that God does not force us to take the path which we are supposed to take to get to where we should be. Instead, he gives us two paths one path has resistance and the other path has no resistance. It is up to us to figure out which path has the least amount of resistance. If you can figure out that path, then you may still encounter some hard times, but they will flow with ease as you go through them.

I believe that helping families with an incarcerated parent is my calling in life. However, I believe that I took the path with resistance causing my journey to my destiny to be a bit challenging at times. Life is all about learning lessons. What I have come to find is that if you do not pass those lessons, they will keep reappearing and each time they come around the situation is just a little bit more difficult to catch your attention.

While the Baller has been away, my daughter and I have endured several financial challenges as I have had to manage a household on one income. I have had three vehicles repossessed since 2015. The irony is that they all were taken in the same month each year that it happened. The first time the Lord allowed me to obtain a rental car until I got into another vehicle, the second time, I was able to rent a vehicle for about a week and then I had to catch a bus until I got my car back, but the last time that it happened it was as if God closed all of the avenues to make the situation easy. I went to rent a car and was denied. I did not have enough money to catch an Uber back and forth to work, and so I was forced to catch the Cota bus. I had to wake up at 4 am and be out of the house by 5.20 am, walk 15 minutes to the bus stop in the dark, then transfer to another bus, which would take about 45 minutes to get to my job. I did this for about three weeks.

In doing so, I did not complain, and I was not upset. In fact, I was very humble about the whole situation. My only question to God was what am I supposed to be learning from this situation? There is something that God is trying to teach you when he does a repeated situation in your life multiple times. I believe that this was a test of my faith. Normally, I would have been freaking out and stressing. However, this time was different, I did not panic, and I stayed calm. I was able to notice my growth as a woman, a human and spiritual being.

I asked God, to please reveal to me what the lesson was that I was supposed to be getting out of this situation. I told God that when it was time for me to obtain another vehicle, I knew it would happen for me, but most importantly I wanted to understand the lesson I was supposed to be learning so that I would not continue to make the mistake.

Lastly, this situation taught me how to value my finances and to make sure I was paying my bills on time. I have had constant dreams about my dream home and at one point I dreamt that I had just closed on the home and received the keys. However, the things that I was doing with my finances did not line up with the things that awaited me in my future. So, I believe that God set some hardships in place to get my attention so that I could get my finances straighten out so that when opportunities began to come my way my credit will not hinder me.

God has a reason for every season in our lives. Prior to my last repossession, I will admit that I was frivolous with my spending. However, God reminded me of the story of Joseph once again of how the Pharaoh had the dream which meant seven years of plenty and seven years of lack. God was telling me the same thing when things are good put some money aside because rainy days are guaranteed to come. Also, I know that he is preparing me for a prosperous future.

The Baller and I have shared ideas about businesses that we would like to start once he is released. I cannot be the reason that our family has plenty and then lose it due to my lack of responsibility within our finances. I am sure God, tried to get my attention to teach me these things before repossessing my car three times, but I refused to listen.

If you are the manufacturer of a product, then that means that you took raw materials and your knowledge/vision, and you came up with a finished good. Once finished do you expect that product to then tell you what they need or what you should have done better? It is the same way with God. He is the ultimate creator who created us, so why are we not allowing him to lead us through life, instead of telling him what we think should occur in our life? Now granted God wants to give us our heart's desires; and we should tell him those desires regularly.

However, when God tells us to do something and gives specifics on how to do it, we should not allow the enemy (Inner Me) to sway us from God's directions given to us. Otherwise, you will end up living life in the delay. Meaning, God will not give up on what he wants you to do, it is just a matter of time as to how long it will take you to do it. The plan never changes, but we can delay it. Most of the time when we delay God's plan, we end up taking a longer route with more obstacles to cross.

I no longer try and tell God how I think things should go or what I am going to do. Instead, I ask for clarification. We must start trusting our internal GPS, that little small, still voice on the inside of us that is constantly leading us and guiding us through life all in preparation to launch us into our destiny!

For I know the plans that I have for you, declares the Lord, plans for welfare and not for evil, to give you a future and a hope.
~Jeremiah 29:11

Restored: 30

This chapter of my life I would have to say was the most meaningful and impactful. I was finally getting to a point of being able to listen to God and watch for signs and patterns that showed me that he was near or trying to get a message to me.

I do not care where you are right now in the world or what you are going through, by no means necessary, feel alone or isolated into thinking that you are the only one going through your situation.

If thus far in this book, I have not touched on your situation, the principles still apply to you as well. Embrace the pain, let go of it, and heal. Along your journey remember that your higher power is with you, and inside of you. In fact, it is during the healing process that you will actually want to gain strength and inner energy from your higher power in order to get passed what happened to you. Then you can progress forward onto becoming the person that you were created to be and discover what it is within in you that you are meant to share with this world.

If the age of 30 is the kick start to life, then what is holding you back? If you are in your 20s, then are you prepared to put away your childish ways and begin preparing for the next phase of your life? If you are in your 40s, what happened to you that has left you stagnated, stuck, and feeling like you cannot move forward? No matter what age you were when the pain occurred the question is: Are you willing to let it go? Pain holds us hostage from reaching our future. Do you have dreams? Goals? What do you wish to accomplish before you leave this world? Take some time before moving onto the next chapter to answer those questions and then think about this next question: What pain/trauma have you experienced in your life that is holding you back from obtaining the goals of your future? Are you willing to let it go? If so, after you let it go are you willing to start doing the work to start healing from those past/current traumas?

Reckless: Release

The time had come: April 2019. The Baller was being released. I had so many mixed emotions. I still had a soul tie to the Mystery Motorcycle man, yet I believed that I was being obedient to God by cutting off that relationship and being with the Baller to raise our child. So, I had informed the Mystery Motorcycle man that the Baller was getting out and that I had been dishonest with him. I told him that I had been telling the Baller that we would be together when he got out and I did not know what I wanted to do. The Mystery Motorcycle man said that he understood and that I had to do what was best for me and my daughter and that he would always be there for me no matter what.

I also did the same for the Baller before his release. I informed him that I had not been completely honest with him and that the Mystery Motorcycle man was still in the picture up until that point and if he wouldn't be able to handle the fact that I had been with another man, he may not want to come home to me when he was released. He said that did not matter if it was in the past.

The Baller's release date quickly approached, and, on that day, my daughter and I met him at the bus station to pick him up. I was not excited when I saw him. I had a weird and uneasy feeling about seeing him. He was excited to see me, but I could tell that he knew I was not excited to see him. I assumed those feelings were due to me not seeing him outside of a prison in over 11 years.

After picking him up from the bus station, he had about 30-40 minutes before having to report to the half-way house. While in the halfway house the Baller could have a cellphone and made sure to call me every second of the day. At first it was nice being able to talk to him without the phone message coming on stating that this was a call from a federal prison and that all calls were being monitored and recorded or the phone beeping after 15 minutes to end the call. Then he began to get passes where he could leave for a couple of hours, so that gave us time to rekindle our relationship and for him and our daughter to get to know each other as well. Soon, weekly passes turned into weekend home passes. The weekend passes allowed him to get picked up on a Friday and not have to return until Sunday night.

The longer the Baller was out the more I began to see that prison had changed him. He had a problem sleeping at night and would get up throughout the night. When we were in public he would get upset if people were standing too close to us. As a part of him being on a home pass, he had to call the half-way house to report his movement changes and he would constantly be checking the phone to see if they had called or he would call them constantly to let them know his whereabouts.

It was as if his mind was still in prison and he did not want to miss count time out of fear of the consequences. The cellphone he was using was a cheap flip phone from Walmart due to the half-way house saying they could only have a flip phone, However, when he came to the house and seen old cellphones that I had sitting around the house he wanted to use one of them.

One day, he had his first interview scheduled and wanted to use one of my phones. I asked to see it, so that I could reset it to the Factory settings due to old text messages and my call log still being on the phone. He shot me the dirtiest look. While driving to his interview he sat in complete silence. When we arrived at the interview, I again asked what was wrong and that is when he said, that he felt I was hiding something because I snatched the phone from him and deleted my call and message history. I explained to him that if we are supposed to be starting on a fresh start, then my past was irrelevant and that was why I deleted the settings on it.

At this point, he was late for the interview and rather than go inside he sat in the car arguing with me about this cellphone in front of our child. He finally, went inside to the interview only to come back out less than five minutes later. I asked what happened and he said the lady told him he did not need to come because she had all his information. I later discovered that was a lie and he was not able to interview because he had arrived late. This was red flag #1 of a man suffering from institutionalized trauma.

Over the next couple of months, the Baller and I would have frequent arguments. He would find jobs and then lose them within a couple of weeks. This in turn stressed me out because I was now having to take care of him, our daughter, and myself. Our bills were behind and having two incomes would have helped to eliminate some of the stress that was building up on both of us.

I was becoming stressed because I felt by him not being able to keep a job it was adding additional stress on me being the sole income provider and it provided stress on him because he felt like less of a man due to me being the sole income provider

The Baller was set to be released from the halfway house in July. I also had gotten a job opportunity to make extra money on the side facilitating a curriculum. I took th offer, which meant I would have to go out of town for a week. It was nice because m daughter was able to go along with me and attend a summer camp, while I worked. The Baller seemed to have a problem with separation and seemed to have separation anxiety and even picked an argument with me before leaving.

On Wednesday, one of the Facilitators needed to fly back home but needed a ride back to the airport. He asked if I could take him and I said yes. I figured I could chec on my house and surprise the Baller as well. While on the way to the airport the Balle called and when he found out I had my male co-worker in the car and was coming back into the city he was upset. He assumed that I would be coming back into the cit and not visiting him or letting him know and would return out of town to where I ha to facilitate.

Upon arriving at the airport, my co-worker and I were talking when suddenly a ca came speeding up fast behind me and almost hit me, while I was getting my co-workers luggage out of the trunk. Suddenly, the door of the speeding car opened and out jumps the Baller trying to fight my co-worker. He kept stating that my co-worker had told me to hang up on him when I was on the phone with him, which did not happen because my co-worker was asleep. My co-worker made it into the airport terminal safely and then the Baller ended up pulling off. I pulled off shortly after him

I thought that he had left however after I pulled out of the airport drop off, a car jumped out of nowhere and had almost sideswiped me. I looked and it was the Baller yelling at me telling me to answer my phone. I called the police, but then he sped off. ended up going home and no sooner than my daughter and I got out of the car, the Baller was coming around the corner. I instructed my daughter to get back into the car. I locked the car doors and called the police again. I was afraid of getting out of th car due to seeing how irate the Baller was at the airport. I was afraid that he would ge me into the house and physically assault me. The police ended up coming and they arrested him and took him back to the half-way house and stated that it would be up to the half-way house to decide if they wanted to violate him or just hold him there until he was released out of their custody.

This situation upset my daughter who was crying hysterically out of fear because I was scared, her father was acting iratational, and he just got arrested in front of her. She was afraid that he would be leaving her again for another 10 years. I explained to her that was not the case and that I had to call the police for my safety. I could not believe that the Baller would act in this manner, especially since he only had two days left in the halfway house until he was technically free from the custody of the Bureau of Prisons.

The halfway house ended up revoking his passes for two days. I was so upset with him and embarrassed that he humiliated me in front of my co-worker as well as put me at risk for losing a job opportunity that had been beneficial to my daughter and me.

On Friday, it was my last day facilitating and the Baller's last day at the Halfway house and I got a text from him late that afternoon asking if he could sit on my back porch due to not having anywhere to go and the temperatures rising and being too hot to sit in the car. I, of course. said yes, due to having an empathetic heart that sometimes thinks with too much emotion rather than logic.

Upon arriving home, we ended up going to dinner; my daughter, the Baller, and myself. We had a good time laughing and eating as a family. However, upon arriving home the time was getting later, and I asked the Baller what he had planned on doing. He stated he had nowhere to go. I explained to him that I was still upset that he had embarrassed me like he did in front of my co-worker and that I wasn't comfortable having him in my house knowing he still had that anger streak there within in him. He then started accusing me of having a relationship with my co-workers as well as bringing up the relationship with the Mystery Motorcycle man.

The argument escalated into him choking me. Being choked has got to be the worst feeling in the world. You do not realize how much you take breathing in air for granted until your unable to do it and your body is constricted from getting air. He let go and began questioning me more about the Mystery Motorcycle man, but when I answered him, he got madder and choked me again. This time when he let go, I was gasping for air and coughing up blood at the same time. He then took and grabbed me by my hair and pulled me onto the floor and hit me a few times in my head. He then picked up a pair of scissors that were in the room and told me that if I did not tell him the truth about the Mystery Motorcycle man, he would stab me in the neck. He opened the door to see if our daughter was around and when he did, I yelled my daughter's name. I am not sure what I was hoping to achieve by calling her. I guess I was hoping that he would stop his violent attack on me and have a softer heart seeing his daughter. After opening the door and not seeing her, he shut the door and told me to stop calling his daughter's name.

No sooner had he shut the door and there was a knock was at our bedroom door. When he opened the door, it was the police asking him to come out with his hands up. My daughter, my heir, my mini-me part two. She continues to surprise me as she blossoms into a beautiful young lady. She had heard me crying and her dad yelling, and she snuck into my home office where the house phone was located, but she shut her bedroom door as well as the office door. So, when her dad opened the door, it appeared that she was still in her bedroom when she actually was in the office and on the phone with the police. I believe the air conditioner was on in my bedroom, so when the police knocked on the door, neither the Baller nor I heard them. My daughter let them in. He was arrested that night for domestic violence.

While he was in jail the Baller would call me and state that he was sorry and that he needed to get some help. I hadn't healed from the traumatic situation of him following me from the airport and almost fighting my co-worker and now having to process him choking me, which could have led to him potentially killing me I was thinking with pure emotion. When the brain experiences trauma, it can no longer think with the rational/logical part of the brain for it is cut off and the brain is purely thinking with the emotional side only. Whenever trauma occurs the amygdala found in the brain becomes enlarged and continues firing off signals that you are in danger. Hence, the reason why after a traumatic event you're more nervous or fearful and continue to be triggered by certain things that remind you of the event that took place.

I listened to the Baller and felt bad that he was back in jail especially being that he had just come home from prison. I helped him to find a bail bondsman and he was able to bond his way out of jail.

119

Things were good between us for a couple of weeks before the arguments started again. Many of the arguments would be sexually related. He would get upset that I did not want to have sex with him or that I was not doing certain things to him or for him during sex. I soon learned that this was a form of abuse by abusers and was used as a form of control.

After he choked me, I tried to remove myself from the situation when the arguments arose to avoid him putting his hands on me. So, I would leave and go to a friend's house or go to a hotel. During many of our arguments, the Baller would constantly tell me to quit talking down to him or talking to him in a certain tone of voice. He would always say that I held all the keys. When I asked what he meant, he would say that he was paroled to my house and I knew that he could not get in any trouble or I could have him sent back to prison.

Life has a funny way of giving us what we continue to let come from our mouths. I would constantly tell him that he is no longer in prison and I am not one of his old cellmate rivals. He had a threatening demeanor when talking to me as if I were another man he was locked up with who was disrespecting him. His tone would change, or he would walk up to me as if he were going to hit me.

I tried to get him to go to several nonprofits that I knew about so that he could get help with transitioning from prison back into society with his thinking. However, he assumed that I was going to have him go to places to get helped by guys who I 'messed' around with while he was in prison. His probation officer also told him about these mentoring groups he could attend and do the same thing, but he refused to do either. He said that he did enough programs when he was locked up and he was not anyone's puppet in their show.

In the meantime, he was walking around with prison trauma and trying to cope and get back into the responsibilities of the free world, which included bills, a relationship, kids, and trying to obtain and keep employment.

The arguments were becoming normal, but the feeling of not knowing whether it would be a good or bad night brought about fear in me. When arguing with him, I would just remain silent because I feared getting loud or talking back to him would anger him to the point of physical abuse.

I prayed during this time asking God to restore my peace. I told God that if he restored my peace I would be like Lot and I would not look back. Domestic violence has been in every generation of my family, and yet not one of the women has stood up to stop it. I did not want that for my daughter, and I was determined to break the cycle.

So, I took off work one day and went downtown to obtain a protection order. I was granted a temporary order. Once the Baller got served and went to court it made things rocky between us. He was no longer staying at my house because he was afraid I would call the police. My daughter and I got a good night's rest for a couple of days but we were always on edge not knowing if he would try to come in and do something. One night while working my security alarm alerted me that someone was around my house. I looked at the camera and saw the Baller creeping around by my car. I went outside and asked what the heck he was doing, and he claimed he was going to sleep on the back porch because he was tired of sleeping in his car. It was cold that night and he called and asked if I would bring him a blanket. I brought him blanket outside, but the winds began to pick up, and once again I felt bad and allowed him to come inside and sleep on the couch. Little did I know this one moment of empathy was getting ready to cost me a high and painful price.

A couple of days later I had gotten paid and went to the shop to get my car out of the shop. A couple of weeks prior, someone had put sugar into my gas tank and the auto shop had to drop my gas tank and clean it out costing me $700 to have repaired. Shortly, after putting it into the shop I began getting offer letters in the mail to purchase a new vehicle due to my recent bankruptcy filing. I took one of them up on the offer and long and behold, I was approved for a Kia Sorento. I had wanted one of these SUVs for a while now and was so beyond joy when I was approved. However, due to already telling the repair shop to do the work, I still had to pay to get my vehicle out of the shop.

After getting it out of the shop the Baller kept asking me to use it. I told him no several times since I had to give that car back to the bank. Not only that, what did I look like having him drive my car and I had a protection order against him?

That weekend, I had to go out of town as it was the first day of a project that I was doing for my nonprofit organization and my daughter told me that her dad was

121

supposed to be taking her somewhere that day. The Baller's car kept running hot and cutting off and he asked if he could use my car while he took my daughter out. I explained to him that I would allow him to use my car while he had our daughter, but when I got back home, he was to give me back my car.

Of course, this did not happen, and the Baller assumed since I allowed him to spend time with our daughter that he and I were somehow back being cool again. He was back in my house and knew he was not supposed to be there, yet he would not leave.

One day while on my way back from a youth facility I had been working in for my nonprofit, my daughter called and asked me if she could go to one of her friend's birthday parties. When I got home, I took her to get a card and got change for her to put money into the card before taking her to the birthday party.

After dropping her off, I came home and started working on packing up items at home. Oh yeah, so I forgot to mention that a couple of months ago, the Baller took money out of our joint account to go and gamble and he lost the money hence, causing us to become evicted from our place of residence in which my daughter and I had lived at for almost three years. I had no clue where we would be going to live and planned to pack everything up and live out of a hotel and between my friend's house.

Every day, I had continued looking online for places to live, but many places did not accept evictions, and they wanted my bankruptcy to be discharged for a certain number of months before they would rent to me. I tried not to think about the fact that my daughter and I were about to be homeless for the first time in her life.

I tried not to be angry and upset because I know we all make mistakes, but I was furious and hurt. I was upset with myself that I allowed him back into our home and into our lives after getting out of prison. I let him into our lives, and he was doing nothing but bringing us down. It was like I could not keep a dollar in my hand when he was around. I silently prayed to God and listened to spiritual sermons on YouTube: Sarah Jakes, Pastor John Gray, Pastor Michael Todd, and Bishop T.D Jakes got me thru during this time in my life. They helped me to keep pushing through a very dark time in my life.

Even though this man was bringing me down mentally, physically, and financially tried to hold onto my faith. I kept trusting God to deliver me from this domestic violence situation. I kept telling myself that I had to not only do it for me, but for my daughter and her kids, and their kids, for my bloodline. I was breaking that curse. No one stood up for that little girl inside of me who watched her mother endure abuse and no one stood up for my mother who watched her mother endure abuse. So, at what point will someone stand up and say enough is enough. I will lay down my life to make sure this demon stops with me. Well, apparently God was grooming me to be that woman who stops that curse because I know that he has something special on my bloodline, and to encounter it, the spirit of abuse must die.

Now, let us get back to October 17, 2019. The Baller came in while I was packing things away, and while doing so my phone rang. It was a colleague of mine asking if I would be available for a conference call at 8 pm. I stated yes and looked at the time and realized it was getting close time for me to go and pick up my daughter from her friend's birthday party. So, I asked the Baller to move my car that he had yet to give back to me so that I could get out. As I backed out, he called me upset that I left him as he thought that he was going to ride with me. When I arrived at the venue, I got onto my conference call as I waited for my daughter to get ready to leave the birthday party.

After getting her and getting back into the car, I finished up my conference call and started up the car, only to realize I had a flat tire. Someone had sliced one of my tires. So, I waited for roadside assistance to come and put on my spare tire.

In the meantime, the Baller calls, and I curse him out because I knew it was him who had sliced my tire, just like it was him who put sugar into the tank of my other vehicle. He asked where I was, and I just randomly start saying things to him like I was on my way to Cincinnati and that I was moving there. For whatever reason, he believed me and was becoming very rude and disrespectful on the phone.

Thankfully, two weeks prior I ended up applying for and getting approved for a house. I told my daughter that we were going to stay at the new house for the night. She was sweaty from the birthday party and wanted to take a shower, so upon arriving home I told her to hurry up and take a shower as I put a TV and some blankets in the car.

123

I was on the phone talking to one of my friends when the Baller comes from the back of the house where he had been hiding in the dark and he asks, "why you keep telling people I stole your car?" I said, "because you did". The next thing I knew, I hung up on my friend and tried to call the police, but he snatched the phone out of my hand, and I do not remember what happened next.

After watching the videos on my Ring camera, I discovered that the Baller punched me causing me to fall onto the concrete driveway and I must have been knocked unconscious. While on the ground, he punched me two additional times, and the sound I heard myself make while watching the video sounded like someone kicking a dog and it howling in pain. I did not recognize the painful sound that came from me when I watched the video.

When I awoke, I was in the bathroom with the Baller and our daughter and the Baller had a knife in his had yelling at me to unlock my cellphone. I was suffering from a concussion and my mind was still fuzzy. I was hardly clear on what was going on. Apparently, when I hung up on my best friend, she drove over to my house to check on me. The Baller kept trying to get her to leave, but she would not leave. She texted my daughter and asked if she needed to call the police and my daughter told her yes before the Baller snatched her phone from her. After realizing that my friend was not going to leave, the Baller said that he was going to go and turn himself in. My daughter said that he told us to stay in the bathroom and that he put gasoline outside of the door and if we came out, he would light the house on fire. She also said that he snatched our house phone out of the wall, so that we had no way to contact the police for help. He left the house with my cellphone and my daughter's cellphone. Shortly, after he left, I heard a knock at the door, and I remember getting up immediately to go and answer it. My daughter begged me to stay in the bathroom as she was afraid it was a trick by her father and that he would do me more harm by leaving the bathroom.

Upon opening the front door, it was the police and all I heard was the female officer radio for an ambulance to be dispatched. When the ambulance arriving they asked me a couple of questions and examined me before rushing me off to the hospital.

At the hospital, they performed an examination and I just remember waking up briefly and seeing a bright light and feeling them cutting my shirt and bra off me. After speaking to the police, they must have informed the hospital that I was a domestic violence victim and that the suspect was not caught at the scene because I remember hearing the hospital staff say they were moving me and that the whole floor was going on a lockdown.

For people to visit me they had to call the hospital and the hospital had to make sure that I knew them. They were not telling people that I was a patient there unless they cleared it with me.

After spending three days in the hospital and being locked down for safety, I discovered that I had suffered a concussion, had bleeding on the brain, a fractured jawbone, in addition to a black eye.

After my release from the hospital, I had to contact a locksmith to come out to my new house and unlock my door. Apparently, the Baller had taken my keys and my spare key was in my new house. The next morning, my best friend went with me to pick up a U-Haul truck and we went to my old house to begin packing up my belongings to move them to my new house. As we approached sundown, we tried to hurry and get everything out. I did not have time to clean the refrigerator, vacuum, or do any other additional cleaning I would have liked to have done before moving out. We were scared that the Baller would arrive and try and do something. The police still had not arrested him from the brutal assault that he had caused me days earlier.

In the midst, of moving I got a call from my aunt and as if things could not get any worse, I was told that my Grandmother was in the hospital and that she had just passed away.

Earlier in the year, January 16 to be exact, I lost my cousin. She was the first oldest grandchild and the oldest cousin on my mother's side of the family. She was the one who I spoke of earlier in the book when I said, she told me that when I have had enough of an abusive relationship then and only then would I leave.

During the summer of the same year, one of her stepsons also had died. So, in 2019 I had lost three family members along with my dignity, pride, self-esteem, and it felt like my worth.

Over the last 11 years that the Baller was in prison, I felt as if I had found who I was in this world. I was a great mother and doing a great job at raising my daughter in a peaceful, supporting, and loving environment. I had established a nonprofit organization that was growing in the community. I was single mom but managed to graduate from college with a Bachelor's degree while working a full-time job. I had made several accomplishments while the Baller was away.

I had sacrificed my time, money, and resources to go and visit him. My daughter and I traveled all over the east coast visiting him while he was in prison and for him to come out and treat me as if I was nothing more than a piece of trash beneath his feet was mind blowing. I could not believe that he would allow his daughter to endure such trauma. I had worked on myself for 11 years and in a matter of months the Baller came through like a tornado and ripped everything away from me. I was so confused. It was as if everything that he told me was a lie. I felt that I was manipulated and lied too for 11 years. It made me question my logic and rational in trusting people.

This situation would cause me to spend the next several months in counseling and in prayer confused and wondering what the reason was behind what happened to me on October 17.

Restored: Release

So, after reading that chapter I am sure that you were not expecting for the Baller' release to turn out the way that it did. I was not expecting things to turn out the way that they did either. This situation has taken me a while to comprehend. I consistently have asked God 'Why?' I went through an array of emotions. I was incredibly angry, sad, confused, embarrassed, to name a few.

The Baller is now back in prison and my daughter has lost her father once again. I have had time for periods of mindfulness to allow my mind and body to heal from th trauma, but I am still healing daily.

By day three of being in the hospital, the CT scans showed that I had no bleeding on my brain, but I have noticed that I have trouble with my short-term memory from time to time. The fractured jawbone has healed up on its own and I did not need to have surgery. These are things I spoke about earlier, we may endure various traumas, but God is so gracious that we come out not looking like any of it. Working in the lin of work that I do with various families, it has really made me sympathetic to these men and women who go to prison for five-plus years or more.

Although what the Baller did to me was horrific and I do not make excuses for any of it, I do say that I understand his state of mind after serving 10½ years in prison. People in prison for that extent of time, endure a lot of trauma. I am not sure if they even realize the amount of trauma that they endure. They must transform into a whole other person to survive. Their brains are always in survival mode, which is unnatural and unhealthy. That is an instinctive trait as a human we have to protect us but if we are in that state of mind all the time it can cause health issues. In addition, t being in survival mode they are witnessing traumatic events that are resonating into their psyche. While in prison, they are not receiving counseling for what they are seeing and enduring. When they come home, there are organizations that work with them in regards to getting them reacclimated back into society, but they could benefit from some counseling to work through the trauma that they have experienced in addition to working on reclamation back into society.

From my situation, I have implemented a family reunification plan within Unlocking Futures, in which we work with the incarcerated parent a year before they are released to help prepare their mindset for release in addition to working with the family and preparing them to get used to the person being released and being patient with them as they adjust back into society. The parent coming home receives counseling sessions while inside and upon release to help process through their prison experience. In addition, they also receive domestic violence education, coping skills, communication tools, and are referred to an organization to help continue their journey to sobriety if applicable. The family receives communication tools, domestic violence education, and education on what to expect when the person returns home.

We work with the families for six months to a year before the person is released and up until the parents first year of being home. By doing this it helps to ensure that the family reintegration is successful and that the likelihood of the person returning to prison within that first-year decreases, which decreases their overall likelihood of returning to prison.

I never want a woman and her children to experience what I went through. These women and men have served their time. It breaks my heart to see them return into that traumatic environment once again. I do not think any of them want to be there, but for some of them, they do not have the skills or the knowledge to know how to not return.

It is unfair to our children that they must endure a cycle of having a parent in and out of prison. It is also unfair for the caregiver to have to be a single parent continuously due to the actions of the other parent.

If you cannot tell I am extremely passionate about the family unit and its structure. Our society has dismantled that structure, especially among the African American family and that dates to slavery and remains the same today.

Looking back on this situation, I believe there were so many signs along the way that told me that the relationship between the Baller and I had come to an end. We had grown apart and I felt it. I tried to make the relationship work to give my daughter what I did not have growing up, which was a two-parent household.

I think one of the hardest parts about being me, is my heart. I am so quick to forgive and that is a great attribute; however, forgiving does not always mean that you have to give the person who hurt you another chance to possibly hurt you again. We must learn to fall in love with ourselves. Once you are in love with you, you will not tolerate disrespect from anyone. You will realize that you are worthy of respect and because your energy will exude worthiness, you will in turn attract people who respect you.

I like to say that you have to tell the world how to treat you. Otherwise, the world will treat you how it deems fit. Giving someone another chance after domestic violence could cost you your life.

Initially, when I started writing this book, I thought that the Baller was going to return to society a reformed man and changed from his old ways. I am sure you did too as you have been on this journey with me as well as I have shared my story. I now realize that he has some things that he needed to unpack from within that outweighed being in a relationship.

They call prison 'Rehabilitation', but how can a person be rehabilitated when they are enduring trauma daily or having to be in a defensive mode all the time? I am not saying that it cannot be done, because I know men who have done a significant amount of time and have come home to do great things in the community. However, you must have the mindset to want to change and be educating yourself as well.

For some people, they are not as strong and need to be guided along a path to obtaining that information. I would not recommend anyone coming home from prison who has been gone five or more years to come home and get into a relationship.

The most successful people that I have seen come home after serving long sentences have been men who came home, stayed single, and worked on doing what they needed to do to get off papers.

If you are in a domestic violence relationship, please seek help. Abuse is not always physical, but it is also verbal and financial abuse as well.

You should be free in any relationship that you are in to be yourself. You should never feel as if you are apprehensive to speak your mind or walking around your house on eggshells because you are trying not to make the person upset. Your children should be able to walk, run, holler, scream, joke, whatever they feel like doing around the house without worrying about upsetting your significant other to the point of physical harm. Your children should not have to go to sleep at night and worry if mommy or daddy is going to be okay. They should not have to try and stay awake at night listening for signs that you are being hurt, to alert them to go and call the police.

After the Baller choked me in July, I found a domestic violence agency to go to and I began to get counseling. This was the first step for me in breaking the cycle of abuse in my bloodline. I do not know about you, but I remember what it felt like to be that little girl who heard her mom getting beat up. I witnessed one of the nights that the abuse occurred. I remember being scared and frightened and feeling helpless that I could not help my mom. So, now as an adult, I not only wanted to help my daughter to not feel those feelings, but I was also fighting for that scared little girl on the inside of me that no one helped when I was witnessing abuse. So, I had two little girls that I had to be strong and brave for in this situation.

****

It boggled my brain as to why this situation happened to me. However, as I approach one year from the date that it occurred, I am realizing that it made me dig deeper into my spirituality and ask bigger questions. It has caused me to question everything that I once knew regarding spirituality and become open to new ideas. It allowed me to help my clients on a deeper level as well.

Instead of offering them a service, I realized that they needed to unpack what has caused them to get into their situation and start working to heal from that point and working our way upward. Providing a surface level service without getting to the root will only apply band-aids to people's situations. I am not in the business of providing band-aids and temporary solutions. I want people to live healthy lives. I want to see healthy families who will ultimately raise healthy children who will one day be adults in our society.

So, as I bring this chapter to a close my best advice to you if you are in a domestic violence relationship is for you to know that the longer you stay the higher the risk that you will be killed. I know that sounds harsh, but it is also a reality. If you have children, you also must realize the trauma that they are enduring from that relationship.

Once you can get out and get away, get you and your child into counseling immediately. For so many years, I thought that I could heal on my own by moving on and not thinking about it. However, I did not realize that I was just packing trauma on top of trauma.

Next, you must work on changing your mindset. You must go deep within yourself to discover what caused you to accept domestic violence as being okay? You did not wake up and decide it would be okay for a man to physically assault you.

So, take some time right now and think about what happened growing up. How was your childhood? How did your immediate family interact with each other? Did you witness violence? Did you see domestic violence? Were you exposed to healthy or unhealthy relationships growing up? Then I want you to try some meditation or peaceful journaling and focus on what you want for your life. How would you like your relationship to look? How would your ideal significant other treat you? What would you look like healthy and healed? How would you conduct yourself in a health relationship?

Before you start reflecting, on these questions, I would highly advise that you be enrolled in counseling. I say this because once you start doing this you are going to discover some unresolved issues that you pushed deep, deep, down within yourself that start to arise. If you are enrolled in counseling you can discuss these things in your sessions, but if you're not enrolled in counseling you will need someone to discuss these thoughts with to help you to process through those emotions in a healthy manner.

Did you know that when the body is enduring a stressful or traumatic situation the amygdala part of the brain enlarges? This causes the person to stay in a survival mode. The rational and logical part of the brain is cut off. However, if you have moments of peaceful mindfulness you can shrink it back down to its normal size. This has been scientifically proven.

This explains why many women stay in domestic violence relationships longer than they should. She is unable to make rational/logical decisions if she is in survival mode.

As I write this, I am realizing that the same holds true for men coming home from prison. Their amygdala has been expanded for an extended period. It will require the

131

having periods of mindfulness, counseling, in addition to a mindset reset to let them know that they are safe. Once they can do this over an extended period, they too can shrink their amygdala back down to size and go on living as a productive restored citizen in our community.

It is imperative that you figure out what your coping mechanism is and what brings you about peace. You do not have to meditate or journal, but find whatever form of mindfulness that is helpful to you and do it.

When you come out of your domestic violence situation, I want you to come out not looking like anything you ever went through and that is possible to do. My goal is to find love one day, true love and when I do, I do not want to smell like or have the residue on me of ever being in a domestic violence relationship. Meaning, I do not want to have old fears cast upon my new partner. I want to be open to receiving love, being loved, and giving it, without putting limitations on what love looks like due to my past relationships.

The Blessing

When I was in high school, my aunt sent me to live with my grandparents and tha
was the best thing she could have done for me. I received an abundance of love in
that house, especially from my grandfather!!

Since I have been out on my own God has looked out for me tremendously.
Anything, I have lost God has replaced it ten times better. Even though I was a singl
mother raising a child alone, we never had our utilities shut off, we were never
homeless, and even when we may not have had what we wanted to eat, we always had
something to eat.

Tonight, I had to stop and ask God why? Why was I chosen to live one path, whil
other people endure a life of hardships? It was at that moment that the Holy Spirit
reminded me of Rebecca and her having a hard pregnancy and asking God what was
going on and him telling her that she was pregnant with two nations, who would be
born Jacob and Esau. I was also reminded of Isaac and Ishmael. God never forgot
about Ishmael and he blessed him as well, but the promise was on Isaac and he did
not forget about Esau, but the promise was on Jacob. As I meditated on these people
in the Bible, it was as if God was confirming with me that the promise is on me.
Therefore, I was spared from certain situations. Jesus said it best: "The work is plenty
but the laborers are few". I believe that my choosing to do the work played a lot into
the covering and the blessings that I have received. It is always the Law of
Compensation at work, which basically states you reap what you sow.

See, truly walking into your destiny when God calls you will require some sacrifice
I used to believe that hardships were God's way of persecuting you for his sake and
that in order to be used by him it would require sacrificing your comforts and your
loved ones comforts to get the job done. However, I realize now that life brings abou
hardships due to us not understanding who we are in God.

God created us in his image, which means we possess the same powers as he does
Despite knowing this we have allowed society to tell us who we are not and what we
can and cannot do causing us to live at a mediocre level rather than living at our
ultimate and highest spiritual potential.

Have you ever heard the saying "To whom much is given, much is required?" God will give you plenty of resources to be able to accomplish your mission here on earth. Those resources can be a blessing; however, if you are blessed with plenty you should also be willing to give away plenty. Meaning, you should be willing to be a blessing to someone else. I used to ask and wonder why I was going through certain situations, but I realized that going through certain situations, makes you more empathetic to others.

I remember becoming so excited when I began to realize what my calling on earth was and I began to walk in it; however, with it came test/trials. When I am fully immersed in GOD it always seemed as if there were outside distractions that came in and tried to attack my child, me, or my business.

In church, they have always spoken about the enemy, the devil, the adversary, etc. However, what they do not discuss are the Laws of the Universe such as the Law of Belief, Law of Attraction, Law of Cause & Effect, Law of Relativity, and the Law of Perpetual Transmutation of Energy. Although, these laws all have different meanings one thing that they all have in common is that they all are a result of our mind. What we do, what we think, and what we possess within us are all a result of what we produce in our life.

The only enemy that we fight is the enemy within that challenges us daily from doing right and wrong. Although we may not see what God is in the midst of doing in our lives, I used to believe that the devil saw it all and he wanted to destroy us, before God manifests his glory in our lives.

However, what I am learning is that if we spend more time in prayer and meditate on the things that we would like to have in our lives there is no one on this earth who can stop you from having those things in which you desire and God created for you to have in your life.

I recall earlier this year traveling back home from a conference in Raleigh, NC and I stopped to get gas. While standing in line I noticed an older gentleman that kept staring at me. When I finally gave him a nice smile. "You're not from around here, are you?" He asked. I replied, "no". He said, "I can tell because your swag is all the way different". I smiled, and then he proceeded to say, "you have the seed of Abraham on you. Your face is beaming with a glow". I was in utter shock and amazement that he could see such things in me after not even knowing me. For all he knew, I could be a devil worshipper or a non-believer. But it was in that moment that I knew God was present.

Each year I try to read my Bible from the front to the back by the end of the year. While reading this year, I was able to read the first parts of the Bible with a clearer set of eyes and understanding. It was as if God bestowed wisdom upon me to understand things I never fully understood before.

However, after going back and re-reading I felt that I could really relate to Abraham and Sarah. God made a promise to Abraham and Abraham being a man of great faith, chose to believe God and wait for the promise to come to pass. We are all Abraham. God has made a promise to all of us. It is up to us to discover what that promise is by getting in tune with our inner self.

What is it that you truly desire? Those are God's promises to you. Now, you have to be obedient like Abraham and trust God to bring them into your reality as you focus in on those desires, believing that you already have them, by feeling all of the emotions that would come with having that very desire met. Depending on the desire there may or may not be tested and trials may come before it manifests itself, but test and trials will always be a part of the human experience.

This is also known as the Law of Relativity, which means a person will receive a series of challenges/tests of initiation with the purpose of strengthening the light within. Do you realize that there were promises that were made to our ancestors that God still holds onto into our current day and age and has been blessing us not because we deserve it, but because of those promises that were made years ago to our ancestors? I believe that there were some promises made to my ancestors that God continues to deliver on through my life.

I know that this book has been pretty heavy as you have traveled along my journey with me and had time to think about your own situation and the things that you have endured or are currently enduring. However, I want you to look at all the blessings that you have received along the way. How has God showed you that you are not alone in this human experience?

For the next week, I want you to keep a journal and every night before you go to bed take note of all of the ways in which God showed you that he is present in your life from the smallest to biggest blessings that you gave to you that day. Often, we think of blessings as beings something notably big happening in our life. However, if the only thing that you noticed for that day is that you woke up then count that as a blessing because as you woke up and took a deep breath, someone slept and took their last breath.

The fact that you can read this book tells me that you are a survivor! You have determination. It is okay that you may have gotten a little deterred along the way on your journey we all do. You may not have had the guidance or information to make all of the correct decisions in your life and I hope that by reading this book I have provided you with some information that you have found to be useful and helpful.

The Lord bless you and keep you. The Lord make his face shine on you and be gracious to you. The Lord turn his face toward you and give you peace.
~ Numbers 6:24-26

Restored: Blessing

In the Indian culture it is said that the human body is made up of 7 chakras. These chakras play a vital role in the way that we act, feel, love, think, etc. in our daily lives.

There is one chakra called the Solar Plexus Chakra. It is in your upper abdomen. This chakra speaks to your ability to be confident and in control of your life. It also is the place that decides what information to assimilate and what information to eliminate. By opening to this chakra, it allows us to open ourselves up to information we are unaware of—the things we do not even know that we know.

This chakra typically begins to develop around age 14 and stops around age 21. This is a youth's teenage years when peer pressure is on the rise and most young girls start to compare their physical figure with what society deems to be the perfect body.

While writing this chapter, I could not help but think about when I was between the ages of 14-21 years old. I endured so much trauma. As I stated at the beginning of this chapter, my aunt had kicked me out to go and live with my grandparents, I had been in a domestic violence relationship with my ex-boyfriend, then onto another domestic violence relationship with the Baller and I lost my grandfather when I was 19. All those things happened to me before the age of 21, which was a critical time period during my life. I did not have anyone pouring into me with positive words of affirmations or just positive words at all, so my solar plexus not only was not developed, but it was dysfunctional.

I am learning that having a relationship with God is a part of the plan, but in order to really understand who God is and who you are it is going to take some real digging, reading, praying, meditating, and studying. Upon doing your inner work you will discover that you and God are one and he does not live apart from you. So, therefore you are equipped to heal, you are equipped to transform your life into whatever you deem it to be. However, living with pain and the devastation of trauma is not a part of our story.

We are powerful spiritual beings on a journey to get something into the earth as we navigate through life on earth learning how to be human beings. Take time every day to make sure that you are spending time meditating and connecting with your inner being (the God within you) to make sure you are connected. Look into your 7 chakras and make sure they are not blocked so that your energies are flowing accordingly. This will make it easier to hear from God and obtain guidance as to where you are to be and where you are to go while hear on earth.

Reckless: Love

I always assumed that I knew love. However, as of recently I have realized that I have been in love with impersonators. I have never experienced real, authentic, love. Growing up love should have helped the inner me to develop into a strong and confident woman. Instead, love made accusations about me, ridiculed me, and put me out of its home. Love chose itself rather than choose me.

I take back what I said, I have experienced authentic, unconditional love. It lasted the first six years of my life before it died in an automobile accident. Then it was there for me before it died on the front porch in front of me and took its last breath. After that I was flooded with love impersonators who claimed to love me but would always hurt me. Was it because they felt like they could lie and manipulate their way into my life to get what they wanted out of me? Was it that they did not get what they needed growing up, so they could not love me in the capacity in which it would take to cultivate the woman that I was born to become? Whatever, the case may have been I grew up not recognizing what love looked like to me. Instead I found what seemed to be familiar to me.

Dysfunction and abuse became a familiar beast. It was manipulative. It should have been protecting and pouring into the young adult that I was becoming and protected me. Instead the love impersonators were verbally and physically abusive. So, I grew up to be an insecure woman seeking validation, safety, and security from the world.

I developed an inner bodyguard to protect me, which left me guarded and unable to let people in. My inner bodyguard told me that showing emotion was dangerous and unsafe because it would open me up to being hurt by the love imposters. So, its best if we shut down that part of our brain and become numb to people who claim they 'love' us.

Romance movies? Love songs? Who were those for? Love does not exist. Love is manipulative and is always looking for its next victim. It does not love itself, so how can it possibly love me? Since it does not love itself it was bound to hurt everyone who came in its path. Love impersonators only have but so much love in their tank. If they are only coming to the table half full, but I am expecting a full tank, I will never get the type of love in which I desire because they do not have it to give to me. You cannot be filled up when a person only has a half of a tank to give to you. So, it is best to move on and learn to love, heal and repair, so that when real love does come across your path, you can be mentally open to give and receive it.

I cannot stress how important it is to work on healing yourself from a toxic relationship, that be from childhood traumas, relationships, or both. If you don't work on healing yourself you will get into a relationship and depending on with who you will either both hurt each other from unresolved traumas or you will come in and hurt a healthy person or lose that person because of your own unresolved traumas.

When real love finds me one day, I want to be free from chaos and confusion. I want to spend long hours talking about our goals and dreams, I want to laugh until my stomach hurts. I want love to love me as much as I love them. I want love to protect me and never hurt me. I know I said it does not exist, but I want fairytale love. I am believing for real love. I am trusting that the love that I can see and feel is out there and it does exist and it will love me the way in which I am looking to be loved and cared for in a relationship.

The love impersonators have taught me a lot. If you never go through a bad relationship how do you know what you want in a relationship? If your family neglected you or abused you, now you know how not to treat your child because you know what it feels like to be treated in that way. You also know what that pain feels like and you can be an advocate to help other children. Although, people can be mean and cruel at times, it's those situations that allow us to feel and give empathy to others.

We must learn to look deeper than the situation itself to see what its meaning is in our life. What purpose does it serve and what can you gain from it? They say there's beauty in your brokeness and God will give you beauty for ashes! The beauty is what you do after the situation. How you were able to overcome and persevere from it. There is even more beauty when you survive and help others who are in the same situation you overcame.

I have survived my situation. I have started the nonprofit to help others, but I still do not feel I have received everything that I need to be able to really help the population that I am meant to serve. I still believe there is some additional healing that I need to do as well. So, I am committing to discovering myself by going into a cocoon like a caterpillar and doing the inner work on myself. I want my inner being and the source which is the Universe to connect with me and when I come out of my cocoon I want my light, and my passion to shine so bright that it blinds you. I want to help as many people as I can to be able to dig deep within and find their light that is on the inside of them to rise to the surface so that they too can begin to pour their gi out into the world and we can make that a domino effect.

Could you imagine what our world would look like if we all gave our gift to the world and changed lives? Now that would be amazing, and I do not think that it is impossible. So, I will start first.

Stay tuned to my manifestation from a caterpillar into a morphed butterfly.

Restored: Love

I never realized the beautiful process of nature until recently.

At the beginning of this book I was 33. I am now 36. I have grown so much in three years. Trauma, drama, and adversity has forced me to seek a deeper knowledge regarding spirituality, creation, and the human experience.

My growing is not quite finished, but I can appreciate the whole process of a caterpillar and the process of it morphing into a butterfly. A caterpillar hatches from an egg and within two weeks it goes into a cocoon It remains in there for 9-14 days before emerging as a beautiful butterfly. Throughout this book I was a caterpillar. I am now wrapping myself up and going into a cocoon and unlike the caterpillar I will remain in this cocoon until the universe decides it is time for me to emerge. During this process I am letting go of old thinking and beliefs, I am learning who I am, what I want and need, valuing myself and for the first time I am learning that I am love. I was created in love from love and I will emerge a beautiful butterfly in human form full of love. It is then and only then that I can accept the love of a partner and know the difference between what is healthy and unhealthy. It is then and only then that I can give of myself fully and learn to trust again and know that it is okay to let my guard down and be vulnerable with the right person.

I made a vow to discover the best version of myself and I am proud to say that I have held true to that promise. This has been an exhilarating journey as I learn things about myself daily. Sometimes they are good things that I am proud of and sometimes they are things that I am not proud of, but I am happy that I am aware enough to notice them.

I still have not given up on the notion of wanting to be married and have more children, even though it would mean being vulnerable to love and that is still scary to me. Being vulnerable to love means that I would have to open myself up to possibly being hurt.

I try to remind myself that if I go into something thinking negative than the energy from my thoughts will manifest a negative situation; however, if I remain positive and optimistic then I will have positive results.

I also try and remind myself that the universe is love and we are God in manifeste human form meaning we should exude love. If we are working on ourselves our energy and vibrations must change as well, which means you will attract the same energy in which you are giving off. So, if I am giving off a positive energy of love and I have meditated and told the universe what I wanted in a spouse, I must receive wha I asked for its Universal Law.

I want to attract a love that listens to my wishes, desires, goals, ambitions and it guides me, advises me, and cheers me on. I am open to the type of love that wants th best for me and is determined to stand by my side and get into my cocoon of transformation with me to help me morph into the beautiful, conscious butterfly that I am looking to become in this world. I want love right beside me as I discover there is no reason to fear anything and no need to hold back feelings. I want love to be vulnerable with me. I want love to love the deepest parts of me. The inner me. I want to find it easy to fall in love with love . I know I said it previously, but I want love to make me laugh non-stop as we create new fond memories together. I want love to hold me accountable, so that I can continue to become the best version of myself by exposing my weaknesses to me in love.

I want to give love a perfect version of myself. Yes, I said perfect. I no longer believe in the notion that nobody is perfect. Who said that you are not capable or abl to be perfect? To say that no one is perfect does not give humanity much to strive fo and it makes us all seem so mundane and ordinary. So, yes now you know perfection does exist and you can be perfect too. The beautiful part about being perfect is that it is not determined by anyone but you. You determine what perfect is to you. Your job every day is to wake up and strive to reach the goal of perfection that you set out for yourself. You are the only one who can determine if your perfect or not and as I have stated throughout this book, your words have power so be the one to empower yourself and show the world who you are in every aspect of your waking life.

Made in the USA
Las Vegas, NV
01 September 2021